BURSTING WITH HAPPINESS

LISA DIMINO WHITE

To my mom, whose kindness, patience,
and acceptance
leave me in awe each and every day.

Contents

INTRODUCTION

I'm not a Pollyanna—I'm really not. I know that some people and situations suck, like right now. As I write this, we're in the midst of COVID-19, which totally sucks. But my nature is to always turn lemons into lemonade, and since I've always believed that I have at least one book in me, why not crank it out now? You see, I've always been a positive person; I've always had the ability to find the small ray of sunshine on an otherwise cloudy day. In fact, someone once told me that I made them nauseated by my happiness, but I didn't take it too personally. I just told her to take some Pepto.

But lately, amid this COVID situation, I'm having a hard time finding happiness, joy, and positivity. I'm struggling with feelings of negativity, fear, and anxiety. I feel like I have to do something to help myself and others during this difficult and divisive time. But what can I do? After all, I'm only one person. Well, I can write, so I'm writing this book to remind myself of all the things that bring me joy and to inspire others to find more joy in their lives too, during both sucky and not-so-sucky times.

Full disclosure: I'm really quite ordinary. I didn't survive a life-threatening disease, or climb Mount Everest, nor do I have an amazing Celine Dion-like voice. I'm a regular forty-something mother of two, living in a suburb of Denver, Colorado. I have over twenty years of experience in marketing and communications management in the nonprofit, association, and corporate sectors, and I have learned a lot from some pretty great people over the years. I recently started my own consulting firm to do more of what I love, which includes connecting with others, writing, and empowering my fellow human beings to find more joy in their lives.

The one thing about me that isn't ordinary is my outlook on life, including my enduring optimism, and my passion for helping people. Simply stated, I have the desire to make the world a better place. I'm not saying that I have everything figured out, but in my more than four decades on this planet, I've identified how to live a pretty joyful life and I want to empower others to find the same joy. I believe we owe it to ourselves to be the happiest versions of ourselves. Everyone in your sphere (family, friends, colleagues, acquaintances, and even strangers) benefits when you can present a more joyful version of yourself. And the best part is that it's all within your reach.

I believe that in order to be happy, we must incorporate regular "bursts of joy" into our daily lives. Sometimes other people create bursts for us, which is lovely, but we can't depend on others all the time. We are responsible for creating our own whenever we can, and the more we create, the happier we'll be. In the following chapters, I'll share with you what brings me those bursts of joy with the hope of inspiring you to discover more of your own.

Burst of Joy #1: Bravery

*I DECIDE HOW TO LIVE MY LIFE.
AND I REFUSE TO LET IT BE IN FEAR.*

"I'll have a small Strawberry Surf Rider," I said, salivating. It was late June. I was hot, and seven months pregnant to boot.

"Sure thing!" the young and way-too-perky Jamba Juice employee exclaimed. "Coming right up!"

I moved over to so that the people in line behind me could order. I was on my lunch break, enjoying some alone time before having to get back to the office. My mind wandered to everything that was on my agenda for the rest of the day: a couple of meetings, a conference call, and a visit to Target on my way home to pick up a few more items for the baby's room. Baby David was due on August 20th, and the date was coming up quickly.

"Lisa!" the Jamba Juice fella shouted. I waddled my way over to the counter to pick up my fruity treat.

Pulling the paper off of the straw and slipping it into the cup, I took that first sip of icy deliciousness.

"Wow," a gentleman in line said, looking at my hand. "I'd hate to see the other guy."

My blood ran cold, his words shaking me.

He was making conversation—had only made a joke—and was certainly not intending to be offensive in any way. And I wasn't offended. However, I was embarrassed. He was referring to the Band-Aids on my knuckles. I had been washing my hands so much that they were constantly bloody. When they got really bad, I would put Neosporin and Band-Aids on to help them heal. I also thought that the Band-Aids would keep people from noticing them . . . *Ha!* But of course, people noticed, and here was a complete stranger pointing that out, pointing out that I had a problem. He was inferring that I'd been in a fight. Little did he know that I was in a fight—with myself.

Fear and anxiety were not new to me: I'd had to deal with them on and off for my entire life. I was diagnosed with anxiety and Obsessive-Compulsive Disorder just a decade earlier, but struggled with fear since I was a kid. When I got home that evening I acknowledged that I needed to get help before David was born. I needed to come up with a plan. I researched doctors and nearby support groups for people suffering from OCD. I was going to fight this head-on, as I had years before when my symptoms reappeared about a year after getting married. I emailed the support group leader and told him that I'd be at the meeting later that week. I also made an appointment with a doctor.

* * *

The Beginning

I watched as my dad replaced his watch battery at the kitchen table. Wow, I thought, that battery is really small. What if he accidentally leaves it on the table without realizing it? And then, what if it gets mixed in with the mashed potatoes tonight at dinner and someone swallows it? Will they die? That would be terrible. And down the rabbit hole I would go. I made these kinds of leaps all the time. I worried about everything, even when there was nothing to worry about.

I questioned my dad for hours about the battery: "Are you sure there's no chance that you left it on the table?" "Do you think you should wash your hands after touching it, since maybe it left some kind of battery residue on them, and then whatever you touch will have that residue on it?" "Can you double-check to make sure that it's still in your watch?" and on and on and on. It soon became clear to my poor parents that I had some serious issues.

I was seven years old and was terrified that something bad was going to happen to someone in my family or me.

Here's a sampling of what else was going on in my head:

- Noticing a staple on the floor underneath my desk, my throat instantly got scratchy. I was convinced that I had somehow swallowed it WHILE I COULD STILL SEE IT ON THE FLOOR.
- I just knew that either my brother or I would get kidnapped at the mall.
- I wanted to stop my parents from going out on dates because there would be a terrible car crash, and they would die.
- I always looked under my bed to make sure that a fire hadn't started under there.
- I made sure that my hands were completely dry before turning a light switch off because if they were even the slightest bit damp, I would be electrocuted.
- I checked and rechecked all of the doors to the house to make sure they were locked.
- I wouldn't fly because there was a chance the plane would crash.
- Worrying that someone would come into our house at night, I even developed a system to monitor this. Thinking that a vase on the coffee table downstairs was expensive, I reasoned that a

burglar would surely steal it. If I left my
bedroom and leaned over the staircase railing
across the hall from my room, I could see the
vase. My theory was that as long as the vase was
still there, a burglar couldn't be in the house.
(The reality was that my mom probably got the
vase at Kmart for ten bucks.)
- Thinking that every ache or pain I felt meant that I
was dying, I developed a system for this too. I
would intentionally fall asleep with my hand on my
chest so that if my heart stopped, I could scream
and my parents would come in and save me.

As you can see, I believed, down to my very core,
that the world was a very scary and dangerous place. My
poor parents tried everything; they even had me talk to a
nun at our church. Sister Mary Ann was a very kind lady,
and I remember her telling me, "God doesn't want you
to be so worried all the time." Her words helped, but
only temporarily.

Mom and Dad had me go see a clinical psychologist
who specialized in working with kids. I knew her as Dr.
C., and she was wonderful. I looked forward to each
session mostly because we would play board games
during our time together. I didn't realize I was getting
therapy because it just seemed like she and I were
chatting. In her office she had a cabinet filled to the brim
with all sorts of awesome games – checkers, Sorry!,
Payday, and The Game of Life. When she would call me
in from the waiting room I'd head straight to that

cabinet, scope out the inventory and decide which one we'd be playing that day. I'd set up the gameboard, line up all the pieces and she'd join me on the floor to play.

After we each took a few turns rolling the dice or spinning the wheel she would casually ask how things were going. She'd weave into the conversation tips and strategies for navigating my fears. For example, after telling her about how I thought every twinge or pain I felt meant I was dying and the only thing that made me feel better was to seek reassurance from my mom, she challenged me to resist going to her each time something came up. Instead she had me write down my concern on a small piece of paper and put it in a bowl. I guess she was having me write them down instead of getting that reassurance so that I would eventually realize that nothing bad happened, even without having to tell my mom about each worry. It did help.

A lot of what she would tell me were the same things my parents had told me hundreds of times before, but hearing her say them made more of an impact. Essentially, I believed her because she was a stranger. Whether true or not, I knew that my parents would tell me whatever they could to make me feel better, but Dr. C. didn't have to do this, so what she said carried more weight. Since she had no skin in the game, I felt that she could be more objective than my parents.

Little by little, I started to feel better. I spent less time worrying and more time playing, or just being a kid. For the most part, I no longer obsess over my worries or fears.

Here We Go Again

All through high school and college I was fine. Occasionally I would worry about things that came up, but nothing extreme or problematic. But when I got married everything went sideways again. When I was young, my obsessions focused mostly on me or someone I loved becoming ill, being harmed, or dying. Now, in addition to those fears, I became somewhat of a germaphobe. My worries branched out to include contamination issues, such as dirt, germs, urine, feces, blood, and chemicals. Yes, you read that right . . . In addition to germs, I also feared the chemicals in cleaners that were meant to kill them. I was a hot mess.

Some of my issues included people who wore their shoes in my house *(so many germs)*, touched the bottom of their shoes *(still so many germs)*, or did not wash their hands after using the bathroom *(so gross)*. I also worried about touching a credit card pin pad when checking out at a store *(because, as we established, people don't always wash their hands after using the bathroom)* and cooties in the seats at movie theaters *(they probably never deep clean them—seems like a prime way to get head lice)*, just to name a few. Oh, and porta potties . . . Oh god, I would avoid using a porta potty at all costs. Remember about fifteen years ago when a Dave Matthews Band tour bus driver accidentally dumped human waste from a bridge onto a tour boat full of people traveling on the Chicago River? I remember hearing that story and instantly getting short of breath: talk about a germaphobe's worst nightmare.

To combat my fears, I would compulsively clean and wash with a cleaner that I deemed to be "safe" (one that didn't contain strong chemicals) or with plain old soap and water. I would wash my hands for several minutes and avoid touching objects and going into places that I thought were "contaminated." I also continued to have strong urges to check and double-check doors to ensure they were locked, especially since I no longer lived at my parents' house. Growing up, my dad was the official "checker" of the locks in our home (although I played a significant supporting role.) Now, in the home that my new husband Jonathan and I shared, I was in charge of it. Jonathan was much more laid back when it came to those things.

I was also afraid of unintentionally hurting someone. For example, while I loved having friends or family over for dinner, it also caused a lot of stress because I was afraid I would undercook something or accidentally touch raw chicken and then touch something else while preparing the meal and end up giving everybody salmonella. Every once in a while, I would even drive around a parking lot or circle the neighborhood a couple of times if I felt a "bump" under the tires to ensure that I hadn't hit something—or someone.

I tended to make extreme connections between events. For example, if someone touched something that I believed to be contaminated, and then that person touched someone or something else, that secondary person/place/thing was now contaminated too, and so on. The endless chain of events was mentally exhausting. If washing my hands once was good, then washing them twice was better. And three times was even better than that. You get the idea.

A few months after we got married, I noticed that both my fear of germs and my extreme handwashing habit were starting again. In addition, irrational fears were entering into my head, and I was struggling to get them under control. Things came to a head one afternoon when I was in a Burger King bathroom and inadvertently dropped my keys on the floor. I was paralyzed. *Oh no. What do I do?* I needed my keys to drive home, but I was terrified of all the germs on them—you know how gross fast food bathroom floors are. I picked up the keys with a paper towel, wrapping it around them until I could get them home to scrub them clean.

Later that week, I dropped some change on the floor near a vending machine. Fearing the dirty, germy floor, I was too scared to pick up the coins, so I left them there and walked off. As I got a few steps away, I noticed a guy walking by who saw the coins. I turned around and watched in awe as he stooped down, picked them up, put them in his pocket, and then casually strolled away. He may have even been whistling a little tune as he did it. I was so jealous of him. *What must it be like to not even think about the disgusting floor?* He just thought it was his lucky day.

Around that time, I also remember shopping at a grocery store and noticing that one of the carts had some sort of weird white powder on it. It looked like laundry detergent, but I couldn't confirm it because I certainly wasn't going to touch it or get too close. From that day forward, I never used another cart when shopping at that grocery store, afraid that with my luck that I would end up with that specific cart. Even if it had been cleaned, there might still be small traces of whatever it was left on there. I made sure whatever I bought could fit into one of the smaller carts, or in my arms.

I felt compelled to get some sort of reassurance that everything was going to be okay. If I didn't, I became absorbed in the constant worries that were swirling around in my head. Because Jonathan was there and expressed concern for me, wanting to know what was wrong, I would tell him what I was worried about. He wanted to make me feel better and would assure me that everything was going to be okay.

Because of my anxiety and fears I started to become depressed and felt like a complete failure. I was not the same girl that Jonathan had married less than a year before. That woman had been fun, lighthearted, and spunky. This girl was nervous, worried, scared, and insecure. I'm sure he wished that our marriage had come with a money-back guarantee. I knew I had to figure something out because I was miserable, and clearly not living the life I wanted. I looked up Dr. C. on the off chance that she was still practicing. She was, and I made an appointment.

During our first meeting, I reminded her that she had helped me fifteen years earlier and that I was hoping she could help me now. In addition to my fear and anxiety issues, we determined that I was also struggling with Obsessive-Compulsive Disorder (OCD). I wasn't shocked. When I asked why, after all this time, my issues were surfacing again after being dormant for so many years, she said that whenever I experience major life changes (getting married, moving in with Jonathan, etc.) these issues can spike. We found a medication that worked, and Dr. C. helped me with exposure therapy. This involved touching things that freaked me out and learning to resist the urge to wash my hands. Each time I did it and realized that nothing bad happened, the more empowered I became.

OCD is a mind game for sure. The more "successes" I had, the better I got at it, and the momentum encouraged me to keep challenging myself. I built incredible self-confidence and felt tremendous bursts of joy with each successful exposure. I was finally feeling better; my fears and issues were once again under control.

Then, eight years later, I got pregnant.

By then, we had relocated to Colorado from the East Coast. I remembered what Dr. C. had told me—symptoms can resurface during major life changes—so I wasn't surprised when they flared up again. During my pregnancy, I felt so much pressure: it was entirely up to me to keep this child safe until he was ready to come into the world. I was a nervous wreck. If I ate cheese, I had to make sure it was pasteurized because I had read that unpasteurized cheese could be dangerous.

I remember once forgetting to confirm with the restaurant server if the cheese on a salad was pasteurized before eating it, so I ended up having to call to ask the next day. Caesar dressing was out because of the raw eggs. Three years later, when I was about six months pregnant with our second child, Catherine, there was a recall on fresh cantaloupe because of a listeria outbreak. I didn't sleep for weeks because, as luck would have it, I had eaten some cantaloupe a few days before the report came out.

While I was nervous during both preg-nancies, I was much worse during my first. I would get uncontrollably anxious when I thought about what could go wrong after he was born. *How can I prevent SIDS? What about germs? What if he gets sick? What if the daycare teacher doesn't wash his little hands before feeding him lunch after he plays in the dirt outside?* What if, what if, what if . . . It was exhausting.

Baby David

After David was born, I continued therapy, taking my medication, and participating in my weekly support group meetings. The group was helpful because a couple of us were going through similar phases in our lives. Another young woman about my age had just had a little boy too. During a meeting she tearfully shared the reason she finally ended up getting help. She was struggling with breastfeeding and could barely produce enough to feed her son and had to supplement with formula. She felt a lot of pressure about it and told the story of how after pumping for almost an hour she had about five ounces in the bottle ready to give to him. It was a huge victory for her because she wasn't typically able to get that much. She was so proud. When she turned her back to go get the baby she returned to see her cat sitting next to the bottle, which she hadn't covered. She became obsessed with the idea that a cat hair may have gotten into the bottle, so she was afraid to feed it to her baby. She ended up pouring the entire thing down the drain.

With these resources in place and my coping tools in my back pocket ready to be pulled out when I needed them, I actually managed my issues pretty well with a newborn. (While writing this book, just to be sure my recollection was accurate, I confirmed this with Jonathan. He agreed that I behaved like a neurotic first-time mother, but nothing too crazy.)

Of course I was very nervous and over-protective. I remember worrying about David crawling on dirty floors, playing on germy playground equipment, touching the interactive displays in the children's museum, sitting in the grass at the park for fear of dog poop, choking when he was starting to eat solid foods, and that sort of thing. I'd let him do the things that I felt concerned about, but of course he got a thorough bath at the end of each day. But generally, I was able to push through it and allow my kids to be kids. (Like I said, I was better with Catherine . . . there's something about the second kid that allows you to be a bit more relaxed. I wouldn't say I was laid-back by any means, but I figured that I knew enough to keep my first child alive, so I could do it for my second child too.)

Jonathan is my exact opposite in so many ways: much less emotional, more rational, and very level-headed. Although we had occasional disagreements, such as the ongoing one about whether or not David needed to wear a jacket (I always argued that he did—after all, I didn't want him catching a cold), we navigated the challenges of new parenthood pretty well and made a good team. I was, however, adamant that people wash their hands or use hand sanitizer before holding him. (Heck, I'd have had them bathe in it if I could.) Sometimes things rattled me that other people probably would never have thought of. For instance, I remember a friend who wanted to hold him, but she had just broken her arm and had a cast on. I cringed. *How dirty was that cast? It's not like she could wash it.* Stuff like that always entered my mind.

But I was conscious that I didn't want to parent my kids from a place of fear. While my overreactions, fears, and worries that something bad could happen came from a place of intense love, I tried to keep myself in check. I didn't want them to miss out on fun stuff that all kids get to experience because of my anxiety or issues; I knew they were MY issues.

Now

When I noticed my problems resurfacing as a newlywed, and again when I was pregnant, I had two choices: either accept it and say, "I'm just a nervous person . . . that's who I am," or figure out how to change it. I knew I had to change it. I wanted more from life: for me, for my family, and especially for my kids. I didn't want my children growing up with the kind of fear that I'd experienced. More importantly, I didn't want them taking on my anxious outlook, growing up thinking that life is to be feared, and not lived.

If you think I'm completely fearless and living a worry-free life today, you'd be wrong. While I'm so much better than I ever have been,* my knee-jerk response to situations continues to be fear and anxiety. It's a constant struggle to keep myself in check and fight the urge to let worry and the "what if" mentality take over.

Most of the time, I'm able to think more rationally, rather than just freaking out and panicking. But certain things still make me uncomfortable—mostly the idea of people not washing their hands after using the bathroom, and the fact that floors are germ-ridden. I also still avoid using porta potties at all costs. If my bladder is about to explode and I have absolutely no other choice, I will use one, but I'll hate every second of it. I've come a long way, baby.

David is now eleven years old, and my little Catherine is eight. I am so blessed; they are such wonderful and very well adjusted kids, but occasionally, fear shows its ugly head to remind me that it's still around. For example, a few months ago, David came home looking sad after just a few minutes of hanging out with his friends. I looked up from my vacuuming and asked him what was wrong.

* Before COVID-19

"They all walked to King Soopers to buy a snack," he replied. (King Soopers is the grocery store across the street.)

"Well, you could have gone with them," I replied.

"I could?!" he asked, shocked.

"Sure," I said. "Just stay with your friends and pay attention when you cross the street and obey the walk signal."

"Oh boy!" he said, running off at light speed to catch up with his bros.

I went back to what I was doing, feeling like Mother of the Year. *I'm awesome! Look how far I've come!* We live in a suburban neighborhood, and to get to the grocery store requires crossing a four-lane road, but there's a crosswalk signal, and it's relatively safe.

About five minutes after he left, butterflies started flying around at warp speed in my stomach. *Oh crap, what did I do?* Here come those doubts . . . What if a car didn't adhere to the red light when the boys were crossing the street? I started to panic. What had I done? I sat down, did some deep breathing, and reeled myself in. I tried to look at the situation objectively:

- He was with a group of responsible kids.

- He knew how to push the crosswalk button and would look both ways.
- The drivers in our area were pretty cautious.
- It was the middle of the afternoon.

I went back to my cleaning, but I was still a little nervous. Was there a chance something bad could happen? Yes, I supposed there was. Was it likely? No, it wasn't, but I felt tremendous relief when he got home twenty minutes later.

It was hard to let him go, but I'm so proud that I did. That was a big step for me, and the act of trusting and letting go brought a huge burst of joy for both of us. That moment of doubt after he left, however, reminded me that at my core, I'll always be afraid and anxious; I'll never be completely free of these feelings. I wish that wasn't the case, but it is, and I accept it. The important thing is what I do with those feelings and that I continuously work to improve because if I didn't, they would be so much worse. Life's too short to not live the life you want.

Most of us can hide our issues pretty well, but everyone has something that they're dealing with. Friends, acquaintances, and colleagues don't know about my issues until I tell them, and they are shocked to learn about my childhood fears and the ongoing struggles that I still have. They see me as a carefree, easygoing mom, and woman.

That's who I strive to be, so it's cool that they see me that way. It's also cool because it reminds them that everyone has troubles; no one has it as "together" as they make it seem. Obviously, I'm very vocal about my struggles (otherwise I wouldn't be writing about them)! In being vocal about my issues, I hope to inspire and empower others to take control of and to improve whatever issues they're dealing with personally.

I accept that I'll never be fearless—I really do—and I don't strive to be. That would be amazing, but it's not realistic. Instead, my goal is to "fear less." If I can reduce the intensity of my fears by anywhere from sixty to seventy percent, I'm happy. Of course, it varies depending on what's happening in my life (sometimes I'm shocked at how brave I feel, other times not so much). However, I'm realistic about it. And when I notice that the tools in my toolbox and meds aren't working consistently to allow me to live a relatively calm life, I will reach out for help. There's no shame in that. As Dr. C. said, when major life changes happen, I shouldn't be surprised if my fear, anxiety, and OCD flare-up; it's how I'm wired. I accept it, but I'll also be brave and attack it head-on. My husband deserves a happy wife. My kids deserve a happy mom. And I deserve a happy me.

COVID

As I mentioned earlier, I'm writing this book during the Coronavirus (COVID-19) pandemic. I'm not going to lie . . . I've come really close to losing it; talk about my worst nightmare. I've been washing my hands so much that they feel like they're about to fall off. Catherine and I were out for a walk around the neighborhood the other day, her soft little hand in mine.

"You know why my hands are soft, and yours are rough, Mom?" She looked up at me.

"Why, Cath?"

"Because I'm a kid, and you're old," she stated matter-of-factly.

I nodded, thinking that, yes, that was one reason. But the other is because Mommy's been washing her hands dozens of times a day for the past several weeks. My fear of germs and anxiety about keeping my family safe are at an all-time high, as you can imagine. If you had asked me how I was doing only a few short months ago, back in February 2020, before everything went to hell, I would have told you that I'd never been happier. My issues were (for the most part) well under control; I was doing really well. I was taking things in stride and not obsessing as much over germs and dirt, or worrying about other people contaminating my spaces.

24

Now, it's a different story. My stress level has skyrocketed. Once again, I catch myself making mental notes as to who's touching what, and I'm also making those contamination connections: *Did Jonathan use his phone while at the grocery store? If he did and didn't wipe it down when he got home, all the germs from the phone are now on his hands, and whatever he touches in the house is now contaminated.*

In addition, I'm vigilantly monitoring our household members' handwashing habits and forcing rewashes when they don't meet my strict standards. I'm also taking all official recommendations to the extreme. Scientists recommend we wash our hands for twenty seconds? Well, one minute and twenty seconds must be even better! Limit the places we go? No problem! I haven't left the house (except for strolls around the neighborhood) for eight weeks, and counting.

Leave nonperishable groceries, mail, and packages in the garage for twenty-four to forty-eight hours to let the germs die? Okay, so seven days must be even better to make sure those little bastards are really dead. Wipe down groceries and deliveries? Sure, but it takes me an hour and a half because I have to wash my hands in between and after touching each item. I bit poor David's head off the other day because he dared to touch the package of cookie dough before I had the chance to wipe it down properly.

Speaking of wiping down groceries, my concern about chemicals and cleaners is resurfacing too: Is it safe to be wiping groceries with disinfectant? Am I going to kill us by doing this? But if I don't do this, will we get COVID? Which is worse? Death by COVID, or death by chemicals in the cleaning products I use to protect us from COVID? Oh, the cruel irony of it all.

The bottom line is that I'm miserable. This is my worst nightmare: confirmation that the world is a scary and dangerous place after all. I'm living with a perpetual pit in my stomach about what can go wrong.

I'm trying to use my coping tools and everything I've learned to get through this, but this time, it feels different. This threat is obviously more real than any of the other things I've made up in my head and worried about in the past. To make matters worse, I have mild asthma, so of course, that feeds into my fears as to what would happen if I got this terrible illness. My asthma isn't bad—just bad enough to make me freak out more. In all honesty, I'd probably be just as freaked out even if I didn't have it since we hear stories of perfectly healthy people getting seriously ill and even dying. Every time I feel a tickle in my throat, a pain in my chest, or let out a cough, I brace myself: it must be the beginning of the end.

I'd give anything to go back to the days when my worries were not real threats compared to this real one we're dealing with now . . . Back to a time when my biggest concerns were inhaling paint fumes from the home improvement project Jonathan was working on in the garage, worrying that the splinter David got at the playground would get infected, watching Catherine step on bird poop in the backyard, or seeing one of my kids drop something on the floor and proceed to eat it (the five-second rule does not exist in my universe). If only I could go back to the time when those were my biggest worries. Little did I know how simple things were back then, and what was waiting for us right around the corner.

Businesses are starting to reopen slowly here in Colorado, but I feel it's too soon. How about we give it another week? Or two? Or ten? Yes, I'm ready to be released from house arrest, but I'm also very scared; I wonder if I'll ever be ready. I'll probably always think that it's too soon. Small gatherings of fewer than ten people are allowed, restaurants are continuing to do pick-ups and deliveries, and malls, dental offices, and even salons are reopening. I have friends who can't wait to get back to working out at the gym, get a cut and color at their hair salon, and eat a prime rib inside their favorite steakhouse. That's beyond my realm of comprehension, and I don't know when I'll feel ready to do that again.

I'm noticing that some of David's friends are riding their bikes around the neighborhood together (while social distancing, from what I can tell). As hard as the quarantine has been, I think trying to get back to a normal sort of life is going to be even more difficult for me. I'm scared to start living again. I'm afraid of my kids going out and playing with other kids, even if they practice six feet apart social distancing (knowing that kids will be kids and even if they intend to keep that space between them they will likely forget at times). I'm scared to have my parents over for fear that I'm unknowingly carrying this virus and may give it to them, or vice versa.

As difficult as it has been to be hunkered down at home, at least I feel like my family is somewhat safe and that I'm able to maintain some sense of control. Opening ourselves back up to interacting with others terrifies me. But, as Jonathan says, we have to get back to living and take baby steps to find new ways to engage. It's just so hard. So far, we've all been healthy, which feeds into my belief that whatever I'm doing (i.e., washing my hands so much that they're raw, enforcing stringent handwashing from others in the house, wiping down groceries to the extreme, being vigilant about staying away from people, etc.) must be working, so we should keep doing it. But I suppose we can't do it forever.

I'm very worried about regressing. Will I slide back on the twenty plus years of progress I've made and be even more obsessive and worried, now that it's confirmed that the world and some of the germs in it really are dangerous, even deadly? Or will it make me stronger and give me confidence, knowing that I got through this nightmare so that whatever comes along next will pale in comparison and I'll get through that too? I'm hoping for the latter, but I just don't know. I suppose only time will tell, but rest assured that what I do know is this: if my OCD and fears once again try to take over my life, I won't let them. If I need to seek out help again, I will. I know that fear will always have a stronghold on me, but I'm stronger than the fear. I'll bet you're also stronger than whatever it is that's holding you back from being as happy as you know you can be . . . as happy as you deserve to be.

My Challenge to You

What kinds of mental, physical, social, or emotional issues are you struggling with? Are any of them significant enough that they're limiting your happiness and impacting your quality of life, and the lives of those you love? What would your life look like if you could improve them, even marginally? Would you experience more joy if you were able to reduce the impact of those issues?

Once you identify what you'd like to change, come up with a plan, and get to work. Are there virtual or in-person support groups you can join? Perhaps you have a friend you can connect with who can hold you accountable toward making those changes? Are books available that you can read to educate yourself? Or, like me, do the issues require professional help to work through?

Whatever it is, get started. Don't give up! You owe it to yourself, and to those you love, to be the best—and happiest—version of you because when you're happier, you are a better spouse, parent, colleague, friend, and human being. Life doesn't have to be so hard . . . Overcoming whatever your issue is, even marginally, will bring you confidence and *bursts of joy* in the long run. You'll look back and feel so proud of yourself. Remember, everybody has something that they're struggling with—they're just very good at hiding it.

If you're comfortable sharing about your struggles with others, consider talking about them. Not only will this help you, but it also helps others realize that they're not alone, even if your struggles differ from theirs. Once, I was telling a friend about how I felt growing up, and she shared that her son was going through some of the same anxieties that I had as a kid. I could see the relief in her face at being able to talk about it, and it gave her some hope that he would be okay too (after all, even with my challenges, I turned out pretty well, if I may say so myself). I gave her some suggestions regarding what helped me when I was his age, and it made me so happy to be able to help her, even if it was just a little bit. As I mentioned earlier, reaching out also reminds others that everyone is dealing with something, and there's a strengthening of the human connection that comes from sharing our various life struggles.

BURST OF JOY #2: NANCY

*SOMETIMES GOOD ENOUGH
REALLY IS GOOD ENOUGH.*

I had seen those step machines at the gym . . . you know the ones: the revolving staircase that leads to nowhere. You just step, and step, and step. *Pure misery*, I thought. I didn't plan to ever get on that torturous device.

One evening, years ago, as I was walking the track around the gym before starting my workout, I saw him on one of those miserable machines. That dude was hot. Built, but not too much. As Goldilocks would say, "That fella is just right." I noticed that the unit next to him wasn't occupied. *Well*, I thought, *I guess today's the day I get on the step machine.*

I set myself up, and, with a coy smile, leaned over and asked, "So, how do you work this thing?" Totally lame pickup line, I know, but it worked. He showed me what to do, and weeks of flirty smiles and waves across the busy gym followed. One evening, after our respective workouts, he finally asked me if I wanted to grab some dinner. It was a chilly evening in January of 1999. As we sat across the huge, six-person booth at our local Ruby Tuesday, we got to know each other. Within a year and a half, we were married. As Phoebe Buffay from *Friends* would say, "I found my lobster."

A few weeks after we got married, I made tacos for our dinner, complete with all the fixings: ground beef, corn taco shells, shredded lettuce, tomatoes, cheese, salsa, sour cream, guacamole. Delish. We sat down to dinner; Jonathan seemed surprised when he took his first bite.

"The beef doesn't have any seasoning in it!" he exclaimed, and spit it into his napkin.

"I know," I said, surprised. "This is how my mom used to make them."

"You have to put some sort of seasoning in it!" he reiterated.

"I do?" I asked, curiously. "Hmm, well, I could pour some salsa out of the jar into the meat and stir it in."

"No," he said. "That's gross." So, in the short time you have known me, dear reader, how do you think I responded?

    a.   Threw a taco at his face

b. Was offended and stormed off
c. Calmly thanked him for his feedback and made a note of it for the future
d. Cried

You might think that it would be "a," but the correct answer is "b" while also "d-ing."

I was embarrassed and felt like a failure. I was a whopping twenty-four years old, newly married, and determined to be the best little wife (and cook, housekeeper, decorator, etc.) there ever was. Even though I worked full time and have always been a career-driven sort of gal, I also had a bit of a traditional mindset and wanted to be the perfect Suzy-homemaker wife. I didn't particularly like cooking or baking (I'd rather go out to eat any day). Still, I had high expectations as to how well I should be able to do all household tasks.

Some background info for you . . . I grew up with an incredible mom. She is kind, generous, thoughtful, and whip-smart. She is not, however, a culinary wizard. I grew up eating Shake 'n Bake pork chops, hamburgers on the grill, canned veggies, and Uncle Ben's Boil-in-Bag rice—simple. Plus, my dad ate everything that was put in front of him and never complained. When I got married, I assumed my husband would be the same way. *Ha!* I grew up watching my mom, so I knew how to open a can, bake a chicken in the oven after marinating it in BBQ sauce or

Italian dressing, and boil water for spaghetti. And make tacos. Well, at least I *thought* I knew how to make tacos. Perhaps I had overestimated my mediocre skills.

I carried on for years with my subpar cooking abilities and stuck to the basics. Occasionally, I would branch out and try a recipe, even screwing up the ones that should have been foolproof. It hurt my feelings whenever a recipe didn't go well, as if it was a criticism of me as a person. I remember once glaring at Jonathan when he refused to eat something I made and muttered between grated teeth, "You can't just choke it down?!"

A few years later, I received an invitation to participate in a Christmas cookie exchange. The Evite specifically said: "no store-bought cookies." *Really?* I don't bake, but in the spirit of trying, I Googled "easy, no-bake cookies" and found a butterscotch chocolate cookie recipe. It seemed easy enough. In true Lisa fashion, when I couldn't find butterscotch pudding mix at three different grocery stores, I purchased the sugar-free versions. What difference would it make? Well, as it turns out, a big one. Apparently, the sugar is needed to make the oatmeal and chocolate stick together to form cookies. My balls of dough wouldn't stick together and ended up being messy (yet delicious) crumbs. Who knew?!

I panicked. The invite specifically said, "no store-bought cookies." *Screw it.* That evening I went to the grocery store and bought the nicest cookies I could find, and, with my head held high, went to the party. Of course, everyone was very sweet and had a good laugh over my poor culinary skills. Apparently, they all could have anticipated what would happen when using a sugar-free pudding mix if the recipe called for regular. No one shamed me for bringing store-bought cookies, and if they had an issue with it, no one said so to my face. Over my second glass from the big black box of Chardonnay, I realized that even if they were judging me, I didn't care! I popped another one of someone's delicious homemade chocolate/peanut butter/caramel confections into my mouth, and I came to the realization that sometimes good enough really is good enough.

I didn't particularly enjoy spending time in the kitchen, and I had zero desire to improve my culinary skills, so why was I stressing over this? Why did I take it so personally when Jonathan refused to eat my concoctions? Why did it hurt my feelings? Why was I using this one aspect of who I am to measure my worth? How dumb.

For whatever reason, there are things in life that we simply don't enjoy, or that we're not good at. Maybe they don't come naturally to us, or we just don't care about them. Whatever the reason for disliking something, why force it? Unless the task is critical, and we have to do it well in order to survive or function in a civilized society, why do we hold ourselves to such high expectations all the time? Sure, we could take the time to improve our skills if we wanted to, but maybe we just don't want to. And if we're okay with not being great at them, as long as they're not a matter of life or death, who cares?!

If a brain surgeon isn't good at his or her job, that's a problem. For the rest of us, what difference does it make? Is it essential that I be able to cook well, or bake melt-in-your-mouth cookies from scratch? Of course not. At the end of the day, very few such things are essential. Once I came to that understanding, I experienced a huge burst of joy, and my life has been exponentially easier (and happier).

Now I focus my time on other things that I'd rather be doing or learning. For instance, late last year, I decided I wanted to learn how to play the guitar—something I'd always wanted to do—so I figured, *why not?* Once a week, I take lessons, and my teacher helps me to perfect all of the classics: "Mary Had a Little Lamb," "Twinkle, Twinkle Little Star," and, my personal favorite, "When the Saints Go Marching In." Admittedly, I'm not very good yet, but I'm enjoying it, and I get bursts of joy when I get a scale or a chord just right. It's been a ton of fun. In fact, David started taking saxophone lessons this year at school, so we put on a concert for the family at Christmas. We provided a beautiful (albeit off-key) rendition of "Jingle Bells." Ah, the joy of creating memories.

Occasionally, I check in with myself to see if my feelings on cooking have changed, and much to Jonathan's dismay, they haven't. I completely accept this about myself; and as a bonus, I've even noticed a pretty awesome pattern recently. When Jonathan asks me the dreaded question: "What's for dinner?" if I answer with "pork chops" there's a 75 percent chance that he'll say, "Wanna go out tonight?" Score!

As they say, actions (or in this case, inactions) speak louder than words. Yes, it would be nice to expand my culinary skills, but the proof is in the store-bought pudding snacks. The fact that I've never made any real attempt to improve this aspect of who I am over the years, means that I'm okay with it. And once I accepted that, it was freeing.

Think of it this way . . . by investing time, energy, and resources into improving things that you don't really care about or enjoy, you're limiting the time, energy, and resources you have to instead do the things that you want to do.

Meet Nancy

I knew I was on the right track when something magical happened. Around the time that I came to this realization, I was working for a company that used an office-wide intercom speaker system to let someone know when a call came in for them. One morning, I heard that someone by the name of Nancy Goodenough was on the line for one of my colleagues. I stopped typing mid-sentence and leaned over to the person sitting next to me.

"Her name is Nancy *Goodenough*?" I asked, shocked.

"Yep," he replied, not looking up from his screen.

Are you kidding me?! I couldn't stop smiling. I had just come to accept that "sometimes good enough really is good enough." And now this call had come in. The fact that this was someone's real name was brilliant. Whatever higher power you believe in, you have to admit that someone by the name of Nancy Goodenough coming into my life was pretty awesome. From that day forward, "Nancy" became a verb in our household. There are many things that I "Nancy" in my life, and it has allowed me to be more accepting of who I am.

Nancy the things that don't matter, or make a plan to get better at the things you want to improve—it's that simple. Give yourself permission to stop trying to excel at things you don't really care about. This mindset frees up precious time and resources to focus on the things that matter. For example, I would never Nancy my children's safety or well-being, but sometimes I Nancy my time with them and let them go nuts with the iPad because Mama needs some time to herself. (And during the COVID quarantine, I'm Nancying a lot of things just to survive.)

Own It

I've finally gotten to a point in my life where I own who I am without feeling guilty about who I should be. For instance, I am not, nor have I ever been, good at arts and crafts. And I have no desire to be. My daughter, on the other hand, loves nothing more than drawing, painting, and creating. I spent years feeling guilty about the fact that I don't do artsy stuff with her, but now I realize that's just not who I am, and that's okay. She gets to go to art camps during the summer, where she does as many arts and crafts as her little heart desires.

A couple of years ago, when Catherine was in the first grade, she had an assignment to turn a water bottle into Thomas Jefferson. That's right . . . a water bottle into Thomas Jefferson. *What the heck?!* I wish you could have seen the expression on my face when I saw that assignment in her homework notebook. I started to give Catherine my pitiful suggestions, but she didn't need them—that kid knew exactly how she wanted to do it. She had a vision, and I was her personal assistant . . . I took her to Michael's and bought whatever supplies she pointed to. It turned out pretty well and actually resembled Mr. Jefferson, if the light hit it just so. (Check it out on Instagram @LisaDiminoWhite.)

Twenty years later, the taco story still comes up occasionally (Jonathan swears that if I die first, he's going to tell it at my funeral). It also comes up when I overcook something to the point that it's unrecognizable. The joke is no longer on me, however, because I have a sense of humor about it now and really don't care. Typically, I stick to cooking the same old things, but occasionally I will try a new recipe that looks promising. Every once in a while I hit a home run, but most of the time, Jonathan's response is to say that it's "interesting," which is code for "Please don't ever, under any circumstance, make this again." It's fine . . . Most of the time, I'll still eat it (I'm not nearly as picky as he is), and he'll just make a sandwich. It's no big deal, and it's ridiculous that it took me so long to realize that.

Have I been known to burn a grilled cheese sandwich and serve it to my kids with the burnt side down and hope they don't notice? You bet I have. That's what Nancy would do. Get to know her—she'll change your life.

The other day, Jonathan, the kids, and I were on a family walk (which we've been doing a lot of during the quarantine). As we strolled around our neighborhood, I noticed how nice some of our neighbors' lawns looked: lush and oh-so green. Our lawn, on the other hand, not so much. Jonathan isn't much of a lawn maintenance kind of guy and does just enough get by. When I

40

mentioned to him how nice some of the neighboring lawns looked and suggested that he might want to step up his landscaping game, his response was priceless. "I maintain our lawn like you cook. I Nancy it." *Touché.*

My Challenge to You

Is there something that you're mediocre at that you don't really care about, yet deep down, you feel like a failure every time you do it? Then you have a choice to make: either decide to improve it, or Nancy it. If you decide that it's not something you want to invest the energy in to improve, then let go of the feelings of failure you have around it. In other words, if you decide to Nancy it, *really* Nancy it.

Or perhaps you're a perfectionist . . . Does everything you do, no matter what it is, have to be just right? If you strive for perfection in everything, give yourself permission to eliminate this kind of pressure on yourself, especially when it applies to things that you don't really care about, or that don't matter in the long run—and most things don't. After a long day, when you just don't feel like cooking, it's okay to feed the family cereal for dinner! Get up late one morning and have zero time to fix your hair? Run a brush through it, stick it up in a ponytail, and call it good! Don't have time to buy and wrap a gift for your daughter's friend's birthday party this afternoon? Swing by the drugstore on the way to the party and buy a gift card. In essence, don't make things harder than they have to be; cut yourself some slack. It's perfectly fine to not do everything 100 percent.

**You can't excel at anything
if you're too busy trying to be
the best at everything.**

For years, back in the 1980s, my mom implemented a genius plan. Only now that I'm a parent myself do I recognize how smart it truly was. She signed my brother and me up for a bowling league on Saturday mornings. She'd drop us off at the bowling alley for two hours while she went grocery shopping nearby. She said it was because she did it faster without us and since we liked to bowl, it was a win-win. James and I would play three games of bowling, enjoy hot dogs and sodas, and learn how to keep score (this was before computers did it for us). Tons of fun.

Looking back, I'm sure her main motivation was not to create fun Saturday mornings for us, but instead to go shopping without having to hear our demands for the most sugar-filled cereal with the cool toy inside, or boxes of fruit snacks (God, I loved fruit snacks). That woman was off-the-charts smart. And now, as a bonus, I'm a heck of a bowler.

In a world where there are a lot of things I can't do very well, bowling is one thing I'm pretty great at. My highest game was a 252. It was a glorious day. Too often, we don't give ourselves enough credit: we don't focus on and appreciate what we're awesome at because we're too busy thinking about what others can do better than we can.

Think about when you go for a job interview. Hopefully, you go into it tooting your own horn, talking about all of your skills, talents, and successes and why they should hire you. Don't just save that type of talk for professional settings—recognize your awesomeness in your regular life too. Go deeper and think beyond just the typical stuff. For example, are you raising a kid? That's amazing because parenting is a tough gig. You're an accountant? You have my respect . . . I could barely pass Accounting 101 back in college – never quite grasped the concept FIFO vs. LIFO. You can bake delicious treats from scratch? Well, we've already discussed my skill level with that. Do people say that you're a good listener? That's huge because most people aren't. Run marathons? You're a (crazy) rock star.

Whatever talents, skills, or gifts you have, don't just assume that everyone can do them; they can't. It may be hard to believe, but there are things about you that make others jealous. I'm totally jealous of my friend, who has an incredible ability to do her makeup like a pro. She can do a cat-eye that rivals some of the best YouTubers out there. Another friend is an amazing interior decorator— she can turn an empty room into a cozy sanctuary with just a few pieces of strategically-placed furniture and the right coat of paint. It just comes naturally to her. What can you do? Give it some thought and acknowledge your awesomeness!

BURST OF JOY #3: FOOTBALL

THINK ABOUT HOW MUCH TECHNOLOGY
EVOLVES EVERY FEW YEARS.
IT STANDS TO REASON THAT WE DO TOO.

I stared at the invitation on the counter. It was for a neighbor's fiftieth birthday party.

"Do we really have to go?" I asked Jonathan wearily. With a three-year-old and a three-month-old in tow, I wasn't getting much sleep. I had the kids on a pretty rigid routine, and with the little energy I had left, I simply wasn't in the mood to socialize.

"Oh, come on," he said. "It'll be fun. Plus, they finally finished renovating their basement, and I really want to see how it turned out."

"Okay," I said, looking on the bright side. I do love cake.

The evening of the party, we headed over. Right after we arrived, one of the neighbors grabbed baby

Catherine, allowing everyone to "ooh" and "ahh" over her incredible cuteness. I seized the opportunity of not having a baby attached to me for a few minutes to grab a piece of cake, and I plopped down on the sofa.

These were the days before smartphones, so as I scooped a piece of the moist chocolatey goodness into my mouth (I gave it four out of five stars), I noticed an NFL game was on. I never cared much for football—never even watched an entire game. I was the kind of gal who went to Super Bowl parties solely for the nachos and booze. I sat there, zoning out in front of the TV.

All of a sudden, I saw a player leap into the air like he was flying to catch the ball that was clearly meant for a guy on the other team. He ran it into his own end zone for a touchdown, paternally protecting the ball from the others who were trying to swat it out of his grasp. People around me high fived and squealed with delight.

Well, that was cool, I thought. The player and his teammates did a little dance and posed for the fans in the end zone; the energy was electric. As I glanced from the screen to the people on the couch next to me and back to the screen again, I had to ask myself the question: *Could I possibly like . . . football?*

There's always something new
to learn about ourselves,
if we're paying attention.

Didn't See That Coming

During the party, all I was thinking about was everything that I had to do when I got home: give the kids their baths, get them to bed, and clean up the dishes still sitting in the sink from lunch. I was tired. All I really wanted out of life those days was an uninterrupted night's sleep. I certainly wasn't expecting to find something that would end up bringing so much joy to my life.

As I put the last of the macaroni and cheese stained plates in the dishwasher later that night, I gave it some more thought. The following weekend, I watched another game in the privacy of my living room to see if it was a fluke. Perhaps at the party, I was just caught up in the party atmosphere, the crowd's energy, and the beverages, but nope, my newfound passion was legit: I liked football. I watched as many games as I could for the remainder of that season, and I've done so for every season since. I try to work my schedule around games, avoiding scheduling meetings or activities on Sunday, Monday, and Thursday evenings, as well as on the weekends during the playoffs.

It fires me up when I see an amazing play, and it angers me when a great player on my team is traded to another. Although I'm not proud of it, I have been known to occasionally raise my voice, ever so slightly, when a ref makes a boneheaded call or when a player makes a horrible play. And, in what was not my best parenting moment, I may or may not have unintentionally exposed my son to foul language, prompting him to say his first curse word. (I know it's wrong, but hearing a three-year-old say "son of a bitch" in that cute baby voice and slapping his palm to his forehead in disbelief just as his Mom did is pretty darn funny.)

I could have easily brushed off the intrigue that I felt at the party and just gotten up to get another piece of cake. Instead, I recognized that it excited me, and I considered the possibility that there may be more to it than just a fleeting moment of interest. I pursued it further, and—to my surprise—I loved it. That was eight years ago, and I've been all in ever since.

Had I been quick to dismiss the idea that I could enjoy something I had always thought was boring/dangerous/stupid/a waste of time/etc., I would have missed out on a lot of fun. (And, if I'm totally honest, a lot of heartburn. Case in point: Super Bowl XLVIII when the Seahawks beat the Broncos 43-8. As painful as it was, I've remained a Broncos fan.) I'm so glad I was open to the possibility that I could be into it, and that I gave it another chance by watching another game. I figured, *what's the harm in giving it another try?*

It was a pretty low-risk experiment. If I didn't like it, I could turn it off. But I liked it. Actually, I loved it. It made me happy (or mad, depending on which team won). It also brought, and continues to bring, lots of bursts of joy to my life. Every Monday, Thursday, and Sunday evenings during football season, and on the weekends during the playoffs, I get my bursts of happiness. The games give me something to get excited about: a ray of light to look forward to when I drag myself out of bed on a Monday morning.

If we assume that we know all there is to know about ourselves, we could be right . . . but if we're wrong, we risk missing out on some pretty great stuff.

Before this realization, I never considered that there may be things about me that I didn't know. After all, who knows me better than me? So often, however, we have blinders on. We just focus on what needs to get done; we do it, and we move on to the next thing. Now, I realize that I'm always evolving. The things I used to like or dislike and prefer or despise in the past may be different from what I like/dislike/prefer/despise today. Simply put, who I used to be isn't necessarily who I am now.

So the broader questions became: *Are there other things out there that could bring me more bursts of joy that I just don't know about? Are there other truths about who I am now that I'm not aware of?* Do any of us really know the current version of ourselves, or are we holding on to who we were five, ten, or even twenty years ago, assuming we haven't changed? While there are core elements of who we are that may not have changed, there are also things that have evolved, but often, we're too busy to notice.

Grayer Than I Thought

In addition to what brings "current you" joy now versus what used to do it for you, your personal truths may have evolved over time as well. For instance, I've always supported capital punishment. In fact, during that first date with Jonathan we talked about how most things in life have a lot of gray area. Except, we both said in unison, on one issue – capital punishment. On that, there was clearly a right and wrong perspective.

He was on one side and I was on the other. We handled it well and engaged in a pleasant debate (obviously, or there wouldn't have been a second date!) Understandably, he felt that taking a life was wrong, pure and simple and under no circumstances was it okay for the justice system to order someone to be put to death. I, on the other hand, firmly believed in an "eye for an eye" mentality and if someone takes someone else's life they should pay with their own.

I had established my stance on this issue in my late teens, and it always felt right to me. I kept that opinion for years, until I was forced to question it fifteen years later. I was called for jury duty for what turned out to be a death penalty case. In a nutshell, the defendant was accused of killing a prison security guard. He wasn't denying that he did it. The prosecutor was pushing for the death penalty, so of course he really wanted me as a juror. The victim's family, on the other hand, was actively protesting against the death penalty for the accused. For the person who killed their son/brother/uncle, etc. Talk about hard to digest. The fact that the family of the person who was killed wanted mercy on the defendant was shocking to me.

Sitting there in the jury box as I went through the selection process, I knew exactly how I felt about this case. The judge entered the courtroom and I stood up until he took his seat. The defendant sat across the courtroom next to his attorneys; he was in his upper 20s, I'd say. The lead defense attorney would have been perfect for the role of slick attorney in one of those made-for-tv movies on the Lifetime Channel back in the 1990s. His silver hair was gelled back and he was wearing an expensive gray suit. The prosecutor stood up, called my name, and started asking questions.

"How would you feel if someone murdered someone you loved?"

"Angry," I responded. What a stupid question.

"Would you be open to the possibility of sentencing someone to death?"

"Yes."

I could see him mentally checking the boxes off in his head.

Then, over the next couple of days both sides dove into the facts of the case. On the afternoon of day three I felt a strange sensation in my stomach. Was it nerves? No. Dread? No. Hunger? No, I had plenty of protein that morning. Holy crap . . . it was doubt.

But Why?!

Why on earth would I feel doubt? I've been comfortable with my position on this issue since I was 18 years old. And never wavered. I believed in justice, and by God, this was justice.

Once I identified it as doubt, my head started to spin. It was so unexpected, yet there it was. How was this possible? Then it occurred to me:

Who I am *now* may be different from who I've always been.

Wow. Just like I used to think football was stupid, I now realized that my feeling on this may have changed too. Or at least evolved to allow me to see that there are two sides to this complex issue. Maybe there's not a "right" or "wrong" answer; there may indeed be some shades of gray.

I was the second-to-last potential juror to be dismissed the day before the trial was scheduled to start. I was so glad . . . for a couple of reasons. First, it was expected to last at least a month long, which would have been a pain in the neck. As I left the courtroom and searched for my car in the crowded parking lot I realized the more significant reason: if the family of the victim didn't want to see this person put to death, who was I to say that he should be? Was it really my place to make that decision?

I realized from this experience that very few things in life are black and white; there's a whole lot of gray area. Much more than I thought. By acknowledging the possibility that my stance on this heavily-debated issue may have changed, I also realized that the world is much simpler when we're younger. We come up with these positions and stances on issues using the best information we have at the time. In my case, I had very little real-life experience as an eighteen-year-old kid. Once I was put into the situation where my opinion really mattered, and

I could see first-hand how complicated it was, I was forced to consider all sides of the argument.

I've evolved, changed, grown—certainly since I was a teenager. But even more so in the past dozen years. Just a little more than a decade ago I wasn't a mom yet; now I have two kids. That's certainly changed my perspective on many things. We're in charge of figuring out who we are now, both in terms of what currently brings us bursts of joy as well as what we stand for and what we believe in. Now I'm open to the possibility that my feelings may have changed on other issues too. And that's okay.

We're allowed to change our minds. That's how we evolve.

Because we believe certain information to be true for so long, it may not occur to us that the pieces no longer fit into the person we've become or are in the process of becoming. Maybe you're no longer that square peg that's still trying to fit into that same old square hole of life you've been living in for years. Maybe you've morphed into more of a circle, triangle, octagon, or a rhombicosidodecahedron (it's a thing—look it up and find a way to use it in a future conversation to impress your friends.) My point is: don't be afraid to morph into whatever shape it is that defines the current version of you.

Two days into the case, the prosecutor accepted a plea deal for the defendant to serve life in prison and the jury was dismissed.

The Importance of Self-Awareness

Organizational psychologist Tasha Eurich writes about self-awareness in her book, *Insight*. "There are two types of people in the world—those who think they're self-aware and those who actually are."[1]

She goes on to discuss the benefits of self-awareness. "There is strong scientific evidence that people who know themselves and how others see them are happier. They make smarter decisions. They have better personal and professional relationships. They raise more mature children. They're smarter, superior students who choose better careers. They're more creative, more confident, and better communicators. They're less aggressive and less likely to lie, cheat, and steal. They're better performers at work who get more promotions. They're more effective leaders with more enthusiastic employees. They even lead more profitable companies."[2]

In the spirit of true self-awareness, I've spent time over the years reflecting on why I love football so much. If you're curious, here you go:

Belief in the Underdog: I'll always root for the Denver Broncos (or whatever team is playing against the New England Patriots). Those two situations aside, I usually find myself cheering for the underdog. I love it when the "little guy" wins, because it gives me hope and reminds me that anything is possible, on or off the field. And in football, there's always the chance that they can—maybe the better team just has an off day, or a key player isn't playing in that game, or the other team finds their mojo.

Hail Marys: I love it when a Hail Mary play wins a game. On Dec. 3, 2015, the Green Bay Packers were playing the Detroit Lions. Green Bay was trailing the Lions 21-23 with time for one more play. Green Bay Quarterback Aaron Rodgers threw 61 yards to his teammate Richard Rodgers, who caught it. Green Bay won 27-23.

Fan Unification in Support: We high five each other like we had something to do with our team's victory, and we mourn collectively when they lose. There's that human connection with people who know exactly how we're feeling—both in good times and in bad.

Fan Unification in Disdain: Tom Brady.

Players Love Their Mamas: Wide Receiver DeAndre Hopkins, who played for years with the Houston Texans and is now with the Arizona Cardinals, has a tradition where he hands his blind mother the ball after he scores a touchdown. The first time I saw this, I cried ugly tears.

Magic: There are so many examples of magical plays, but one that comes to my mind was when Odell Beckham, Jr. of the New York Giants made an amazing one-handed catch in a game against the Dallas Cowboys in 2014. Or when Quarterback Peyton Manning tricked everyone, including the cameraman, when he ran the ball into the end zone for a touchdown against the Cowboys also during a game in 2014. This was when Peyton was with the Broncos, so of course, I loved this play! But I also loved it because it didn't occur to anyone that this old guy would run it in himself, so all the Cowboys were at the other end of the field, searching the other Broncos for the ball, and Peyton's on the other side jogging it in for the touchdown. You go, fellow old guy! (We're the same age, so I can call him that.)

Kindness: The Make-A-Wish Foundation teamed up with the Carolina Panthers to have Braylon Beam, a six-year-old boy battling brain cancer, serve as an honorary coach for a day. The video of this makes my heart soar with joy. There's footage of Braylon showing some of the players his dance moves on the field. They are all surrounding him and cheering him on.

Down to the Wire: I love it when a game could go either way until the last possible moment, especially when it all depends on the kicker. Well, I love and hate it. Of course, I feel bad for the pressure the kicker must be feeling, but mostly, I feel bad for his poor mother. She must be a nervous wreck. If my son David was the kicker, and the winning point relied on him, I'd have explosive diarrhea.

My Challenge to You

Is it possible that you're living with outdated information about who you are now? Turn off that autopilot and think about it . . . What do you enjoy now that you didn't a year ago? Five years ago? Ten years ago? Conversely, what do you no longer enjoy that you used to love? If those preferences have changed, consider the possibility that others have too, and that you've been too busy to notice.

To get the most current information about who you are now, be more aware and open to new experiences that challenge your status quo. Put your beliefs, tastes, preferences, and opinions to the test by being more mindful of situations that arise in your life. Your core reactions and beliefs may have evolved over time without you even realizing it.

If the last time you tried something new was back when the only thing you could do on your phone was make a call, and your watch could only tell you the time, you owe it to yourself to give it another try.

Let's say your pal texts you that he has an extra ski lift ticket and invites you to come along. Even though the last time you went skiing was eight years ago and you didn't care for it (you hated the cold, couldn't stay on your feet, almost fell off the ski lift, hated wearing that onesie-type outfit that made going to the bathroom a pain in the . . . well, you know), what would happen if you gave it another go? Most people would reactively respond in ten seconds with a "Nah, I'm good," automatically assuming that it's not worth the effort to try something again when one's mind is already made up that it won't be enjoyable. What has changed in life that could possibly make you like that activity now? Nothing much—except for the fact that you're not the same person you were eight years ago.

Let's say that you decide to go. What's the worst that can happen (aside from the unlikely possibility of a broken leg)?! Assuming that all of your bones stay intact, you will have spent one day doing something that you didn't enjoy. Big deal. Yes, you may still end up hating it, but then again, you may find that you like it.

Dip your toe into something different. You don't have to keep it there if the water's too hot or cold, but a quick dip never hurt anyone.

As individuals, we're each in charge of figuring out who we are, and what brings us bursts of joy *now* instead of just relying on what brought us joy before. When you're out and about, and a feeling comes up in your gut (whether it's excitement, curiosity, interest, etc.), take a minute to reflect on it. It may be trying to tell you something. Perhaps it's simply that you can no longer digest dairy, but then again, it may be something more.

Over time, you'll realize that some perceived beliefs you have are still correct (I still think hoppy beer tastes terrible), slightly correct (sushi isn't as bad as I remember it being), or completely wrong (football is stupid). What would our lives look like if we live based on current data instead of merely relying on old information?

You can be proactive and actually seek out this information, or simply be aware of it as opportunities arise. It takes some conscious thought, but it's worth it. When I decided to go to that party all those years ago and plopped down in front of that big screen TV, I certainly wasn't looking for a new hobby; I was happy and perfectly content. So many of us don't go through life seeking to uncover hidden opportunities that can bring us bursts of joy. But what if we did?

BURST OF JOY #4: BARRY MANILOW

WHENEVER YOU CAN, DOUBLE DOWN ON WHATEVER IT IS THAT BRINGS YOU JOY.

I love Barry Manilow—I mean love, love, love him. If I'm in a bad mood or in a bit of a funk, I just put on some Barry and I feel better. I may have a little problem . . . I've seen him in concert a dozen times. Most of those times I was in the front section because if I'm going to see Barry, I want to SEE Barry. His beautiful songs and smooth-as-velvet voice make me so happy. I find myself listening to him a lot during this time of quarantine.

A few years ago, I doubled down on my adoration for the legend and became a member of the Barry Manilow Fan Club. I am—wait for it—officially a Fanilow. For my investment of ten dollars per year, I am privileged to have exclusive access to his live show calendar, the opportunity to purchase concert tickets before the general public, and access to his online store containing a plethora of unique Barry products. I even bought a Barry facemask to wear during COVID. I figure, since we'll be wearing facemasks for a while, I might as well find a way to make it not as miserable. (Check it out at Instagram @LisaDiminoWhite). Maybe I'll even wear it when this threat is over. I think I can pull off this look.

I didn't let anyone in on my secret Barry love until more than fifteen years ago. I knew that no one under the age of fifty could understand his incredible talent, or that he really does write the songs that make the whole world sing. Truth be told, I was also a bit embarrassed. Everyone in my circle was listening to classic rock bands like Nirvana or Pearl Jam. Or Top 40 stuff like Kelly Clarkson or Green Day. I liked some of that music too, but I loved Barry.

Finally, I thought, *screw it*, and owned my love of the Copacabana swooner. I didn't care if it was silly or stupid. It made me happy. And by me loving something (or someone) so cheesy it gave others around me permission to own the cheesy things that they liked too. After I told a pal about my Barry love she confided in me that her all-time favorite band is Nickelback. She had never really told anyone, but felt I would understand. You do you, girl.

Right after moving to Denver, around 2004, Barry came to town for a concert. Of course, it was a given that I was going to go, but this was before I really knew anyone and certainly didn't let out my secret Barry infatuation. So, guess who came with me? You got it— my buddy Jonathan. He was a good sport about it, especially since I brought a sign to hold during the "Can't Smile Without You" segment where he would invite someone on stage to sing along with him. I desperately wanted him to pick me. (He didn't.)

Jonathan brought one of the Harry Potter books with him, to keep him from getting bored. So there I was, so excited I could barely sit still, beside my fella, who was reading a book so he didn't fall asleep. We're a match made in heaven, aren't we?

My favorite time seeing him in person took place the following year with my mom in Las Vegas. My mom loves Barry too, so it was fun to be able to share the experience with someone who loves him as much as I do. I was living in Colorado and my mom was in Virginia, so we met in Sin City. He was playing at the Hilton, and we scored amazing seats right in the sixth row. He was in the middle of the beautiful ballad "Somewhere Down the Road" when he and I made eye contact. I gave him a wave and he shot one back to me. Then after he finished his encore I (along with about twenty other mostly elderly ladies) "rushed" the stage.

I held out my hand and he touched it. I imagine I was like one of those teenagers who freaked out when they saw the Beatles back in the '60s. The bouncer/security guy standing against the stage to protect Barry in case any of us decided to climb up on stage, was laughing pretty hard. I asked him, "What, you've never seen women rush the stage at a Barry Manilow concert before?!" He had not.

My Challenge to You

Own whatever it is that brings you bursts—no matter how embarrassing or silly it is.

Burst of Joy #5: Friends (The TV Show)

"It's a moo point. It's like a cow's opinion. It doesn't matter. It's moo."
— Joey Tribbiani, Friends

For me, the best television show in the history of television shows is *Friends*. It's smart, clever, relatable, and just so darn funny. I loved the classic moments of unagi (salmon skin roll), "Go Back to 3B, 3B," pivot, and "we were on a break." Man, that is good TV.

Friends has helped me get through some really difficult times, including 9/11. In 2001, I was a year into my job as the marketing and public relations director for a small commercial airport in Virginia, serving about a half million passengers a year. As you can imagine, working at an airport during 9/11 was tough. One of my responsibilities was to be the media contact, so I did quite a bit of press to get information out from the FAA regarding the new guidelines that passengers could expect as they started flying again. These were the days before social media, so the only way to get news and information out was through traditional media sources.

These were also the days before streaming services such as Netflix or Apple TV. The only way to watch your favorite show was to catch it when it aired on TV, or to get the DVD. Immediately after and in the months to come, I had a hard time not thinking about the tragic events of 9/11: the images that I saw on the news and the stories I heard were on my mind almost continuously. Working in aviation added to my feeling of being totally consumed by it. Like so many of us, I experienced sadness, anger, and shock over what happened. Of course, you know me well enough by now to know that I also experienced a tremendous amount of anxiety and fear about these new, potential dangers associated with the terrorist attacks.

Whenever a new boxed set of a season of *Friends* was released I bought it that day. I hit the jackpot one evening. I was strolling around Target and saw one of the boxed sets on the shelf – the day before it was scheduled to be released. Woo hoo! I grabbed it and skipped to the check out, but the register kept beeping and wouldn't allow the cashier to proceed with the purchase since it wasn't supposed to be sold until the next day. I very delicately explained that since it was on display I would be purchasing it now. Don't come between me and my escape from reality, buddy.

It was so exciting when a new season was available, and I spent lots of time binge watching them - especially when I was having a hard time processing my feelings about 9/11. Whenever I was struggling with the overwhelming sadness, Jonathan would pop in a DVD to take my mind off of it. It was a great distraction and gave me joy because of how gosh darn funny it was, but it was also nice to not be thinking about the reality that seemed to be surrounding me all the time.

A Startling Realization

During the weeks that followed 9/11, I remember feeling a strong sense of human connection with others. I noticed that people were being kinder and more courteous to one another at the grocery store, post office, or when passing on the street. It felt like we were all united in our uncertainty, fear, and anger about what happened. At the airport, as people started traveling again, I saw passengers being very understanding when it took longer to get through the security checkpoint to catch their flights, or when their personal items were confiscated because of the new restrictions.

That October (a month after 9/11), I was in my office when an irate passenger came in to loudly complain about the fact that he was being told that he couldn't fly with his pocketknife. You may think that the knife was a family heirloom . . . That's what I thought since he was making such a huge fuss about it. Imagine my surprise when I looked down and saw that it was plastic and had a prescription drug name on it, so it was likely a giveaway that he had received at some sort of convention, or when a pharmaceutical rep came by his office to promote their newest drug.

At the time of this event, members of the National Guard were stationed in all commercial airports. One of them heard the commotion and suddenly appeared in my doorway. The guardsman stood there silently while this man shouted at me. It was surreal: this man was yelling that he couldn't bring his (free, plastic) knife on an airplane while an armed officer in uniform was standing behind him. I explained to the man that, as he may recall, just a few weeks earlier, our country had been attacked, and that new safety measures had been put into place; he was having none of it. When he noticed the guard standing behind him, he stopped his rant and angrily shouted, "So, you had to call your military man to back you up, huh?" and stormed off.

Wow. Up until that point, I had naively felt that all of us were in this together; that given the situation we were in, everyone would completely support our country's need to implement strict safety measures, and that even though we all felt fear and uncertainty, we were united in our determination to persevere. I assumed that we were all on the same page. It had only been a few short weeks since that horrible day, and the horror was still so fresh in my mind. Yet, here was a man arguing that he wasn't allowed to bring his free trinket on a plane. His lack of compassion shook me—or maybe it wasn't a lack of compassion, but his strong belief that it was his right to bring a pocketknife on a plane if he wanted to, no matter what was going on in the world. Either way, it was my first real experience in seeing how a situation that I perceived to be pretty straightforward, (we needed to protect our fellow citizens, so new security measures were necessary) others didn't necessarily see it the same way. It was a life lesson indeed.

Now

Here we are, nineteen years later, and I'm once again watching a lot of *Friends* to escape from the realities of my COVID fears. I'm also using it as a distraction from the anger and division I'm seeing among my fellow human beings. It's a welcome diversion that immediately brings me a sense of calm and a few laughs. Like my Barry, it brings me some joy and helps me forget the situation that we're currently in.

My Challenge to You

When times are tough, what can you use as a distraction? Find something that brings your anxiety down a bit, allows your brain to have a brief moment of peace, and maybe even brings you some joy. There's nothing wrong with having a few mindless distractions in life—especially during difficult, stressful times. Maybe, like me, you choose to watch a silly TV show, or maybe you listen to a podcast that talks about the latest celebrity gossip or play a mindless game on your phone. Perhaps you find solace in crocheting or knitting. Whatever it is that gets your mind to relax and puts you in a calm space, do it.

Of course, I'm not advocating that you ignore your problems or issues indefinitely and never deal with them, but if you're the kind of person who obsesses over things when there's not much you can do about it (like during this COVID thing), your brain needs a break.

In her book *SuperBetter: A Revolutionary Approach to Getting Stronger, Happier, Braver and More Resilient,* Jane McGonigal talks about how distractions can be a powerful tool for reducing the impact of painful or negative experiences, thereby helping us cope with the pains of everyday life. As a bonus, there may be other benefits to distractions too.

McGonigal explains how research also shows that distractions can be used to control our urges and impulses. Certain games, such as Tetris, can help reduce cravings for fatty foods, and even for addictive drugs. Researchers suspect the cognitive demands of these games redirect our attention away from craving triggers, reducing the painful urge to indulge. Playing matching puzzle games like *Candy Crush*, *Block Puzzle*, or *Interlocked* might help distract us away from digging into that pint of ice cream in the fridge. Distractions can even help us stay fit. Research suggests that by using music or television to take our minds off of the pain of physical exercise, we can improve both our performance and endurance.[7]

Digital distractions and personal technology can certainly help us to be stronger in the moment, but McGonigal thinks they can also help us develop our ability to take on challenges in the future. According to McGonigal, certain personal technologies can aid in building up our courage, with games being a particularly good way to boost our self-efficacy or overall confidence in our ability to overcome problems.[8]

BURST OF JOY #6: BLOWOUTS

THE SMALLEST ACT OF KINDNESS
CAN MAKE THE BIGGEST IMPACT.

Happiness and kindness go hand in hand, but the jury is out on whether happiness leads to kindness, or vice versa. Research conducted at Harvard Business School and the University of British Columbia and published online in *The Journal of Happiness Studies* suggests that kindness has a long and profound effect on our happiness. According to the authors, there may exist a sort of "positive feedback loop" between kindness and happiness so that one encourages the other.[4] I wholeheartedly agree.

When you create more bursts of joy for yourself, you become happier; when you're happier, you're more likely to create bursts of joy for others too. When I'm happy and feeling good about life, I find that I actually look for opportunities to spread that feeling to others, and to build some sort of connection. I'm more likely to smile at a stranger, engage in pleasant chitchat with the lady in line behind me at the DMV, or hold the elevator door open for the mom who's got an armful of kids and dried-up, pureed sweet potato on her shirt, bless her heart (man, I don't miss those days). When we're happy, we're more open to encouraging others and helping them feel a bit of joy too.

Just Say Thanks

A year ago, a friend was turning forty-five and had rented out a roller rink to celebrate. This got me thinking back to my wonderful memories of skating back in the '80s: the smooth floor, the pizza and nachos, the disco light shining in the middle of the rink. I was quite the skater back in the day! Not to brag, but I could skate backward and even do that cool criss-cross thing. I hadn't been on skates in twenty-five years, but it's like riding a bike, right?!

On the morning of the party, I looked more closely at the invitation and noticed that the party started at 10:30 p.m. *Oh. My. God.* I'm usually in bed by 9:30 p.m. (sleep is another thing I've started enjoying more as I've gotten older.) Apparently, for us to have the rink to ourselves, the party had to start after Skate City closed to all the pre-teens and teenagers. I was this close to sending a text to cancel ("Oh, man . . . Something came up . . . Blah, blah, blah") but then, I got a text from the birthday girl. "So excited about you coming tonight! Can't wait!" Happy face emoji. *Damn you, Brandi.*

Maybe it was a conspiracy text because she knew what I was thinking. Or maybe she genuinely was looking forward to my company. Either way, I womaned up and told myself that since I said I would go, I was going to go.

Oh, I forgot to mention this was a couples' thing, so my husband had to come along. He was less than thrilled, but he was a good sport about it. We all went out to dinner beforehand and arrived at the rink shortly before 10:30 p.m. As I stood in the line to rent my skates I tried to remember the last time I was in a roller rink. I believe it was circa 1988, when I was in the sixth or seventh grade. I signed the waiver and the guy behind the counter handed me a pair of skates (the type with the four wheels on each one.) As a child of the 80s, I was feeling quite nostalgic. The rink even smelled the same as I remember–a combination of stale pizza and rink wax. It looked exactly the same, too, only now there was an eight-foot table filled with beer, vodka, and wine in the corner that the birthday girl set up.

I laced those suckers up and got on the floor underneath the disco strobe light. I gingerly made it around the rink once holding onto the wall the entire time just to be safe. All right . . . slow and steady now. *Wow, this is actually fun. Let the good times roll!*

Those good times ended thirteen and a half minutes into my trip down memory lane. I fell backwards, instinctively putting my hand out and landing hard on it – shattering my wrist. Friends skating around me slowed down to help, calling for Jonathan, who was gliding beautifully ahead of me on the other side of the rink. I took a look at my wrist—it was misshapen. I made the conscious decision to not look at it again—it made me queasy to see how the bone was no longer lined up the way it should have been. Jonathan smoothly skated to me, took one look and called an ambulance. The party continued without me while I spent the next four hours in the emergency room.

I had surgery six days later to put in a plate and screws, followed by nine months of physical therapy. *#gettingoldsucks*

A few days after the surgery, Jonathan had to go out of town for work, and I realized that I wasn't able to wash my hair on my own. After several days, I was starting to lose it. I just wanted to feel somewhat normal again and knew that washing my hair would help. Suddenly, a light bulb went off in my head. I remembered that a dry bar had just opened nearby. I had never been to one because it always seemed so extravagant to have someone wash and style my hair without getting a cut or color, but if there was ever a reason to go there, it was now! I made the appointment for later that afternoon and headed over, super excited.

When I got there, I checked in with the receptionist, and the gal who was going to do my hair strolled over. "Hi, I'm Kim!" She brought me to her station and handed me a booklet filled with models showcasing beautiful hairstyles: curly, straight, wavy, updos. "How would you like me to style your hair today?"

Without warning, I tossed the booklet on the counter in front of me and started bawling! Tears pouring down my face as I held up my splinted arm and whimpered, "Please, just wash it! I don't care how you style it. Please, just wash it." The poor little seventeen or eighteen-year-old girl looked like a deer caught in the headlights.

"Oh, you poor thing! No worries—I got ya!" She led me back to the sink where she shampooed and conditioned my hair, and then she styled it beautifully.

Of course, I was utterly embarrassed by my reaction, but Kim was so sweet about it all. When it was all done, I felt so much better, and I looked gorgeous (if I may say so myself) aside from the less-than-attractive splint I was sporting. I left a generous tip and thanked her, not only for the beautiful job she did but also for her kindness. She helped me get through a difficult situation, and—while it was a little thing—it made a difference in my life that day. And I made sure that she (and the manager of the salon) knew it.

Yes, one could argue that she was just doing her job, and we should expect people to do their jobs. But it's more than that. Could she have done her job without being extra kind? Of course, she could have. But she went the extra mile to make me feel comfortable during my little breakdown. We made a human connection, one person helping another, and it was more than just a transaction. Kim showed kindness, compassion, and concern. When anyone does that for me, I make sure to thank them, whether they're paid for it or not. If we all go out of our way to show a little appreciation to those who go out of their way for us, the world may be just a little bit brighter. And maybe, just maybe, more people would go out of their way for others too.

I think we can all agree that people just want to be acknowledged for their efforts, and feel that what they do matters. Your server at the restaurant who traded out the green crayon for the red one because that's the color your kid wanted to do the word search on the menu with, the guy at the UPS store who was super helpful and offered to tape the box up for you when you ran out of tape at home, the clerk at Target who ran to the back to see if they had those awesome sandals in a size 8 because you had to have them for your upcoming beach vacation: all want to be appreciated, and when you do, they will feel a burst of joy. Give them that acknowledgment and tell them they made a difference in your day; I guarantee that it will make a difference in theirs.

If you've never done it, I highly recommend treating yourself to a hair blowout every once in a while. I visit Kim at least once every couple of months . . . life changing.

Oh, and another thing I learned from my roller skating fiasco? Never, ever, drink and skate. It won't end well.

Kids Have This Down

When David was just four years old, I took him to one of those indoor trampoline parks for a friend's birthday party. He was having a great time, jumping like a champ, when suddenly, he stopped. He went over to a little girl who had fallen and was crying. He helped her up, put his arm around her, and led her to where her mom was sitting. Then he got back to the business of jumping. Later, I asked him who his friend was that he helped. His response melted my heart. "Oh, I didn't know her, but she fell and needed her mom, so I helped her get to her." To his future wife or husband: you're welcome. What a great kid.

There's also the time when I went to pick him up from daycare and arrived to see all of the kids cheering on a kid in their class who had special needs. His physical therapist was there, tossing a ball to him. He would catch it or pick it up off the floor and give it back to her. His name was Peter, and I remember it like it was yesterday.

When Peter dropped the ball the first time, David ran over to pick it up to give it to him. While it was very sweet, the therapist said that she needed Peter to pick it up himself since it was part of the exercise she was doing with him. David ran back against the wall to join his friends, where he, along with the other ten kids, cheered Peter on. They would applaud and holler with glee every time he caught the ball, or when he picked it up and threw it back to the therapist. Peter was so excited and proud of his accomplishments. It was the most beautiful thing I'd ever seen. To this day, it still gives me all the feels.

Why, oh why do we lose that sense of empathy for others? I guess I know why … it's because some people grow up to be asshats and don't always deserve our kindness.

But for those who do, and for those who haven't yet demonstrated if they're worthy of it or not, let's assume they are until they prove otherwise. I know some people are big-time jerks, but I believe that the vast majority of people are good and will help others when faced with the opportunity. They're the kind of people who will help if someone gets a flat tire on the side of the road, pitch in if someone is short a few pennies when buying something at the gas station, or invite the guy behind them in line at the store with only one item to cut in front of them when they have a cartful. Consider giving people the benefit of the doubt until they prove that they don't deserve it. When I go into a situation, I assume the best of people, but when they prove me wrong, watch out. That's when the Italian in me tends to come out.

The Importance of Intent

I'm a firm believer that intent matters more than the outcome. If someone intends to hurt someone or be unkind, that's one thing. However, sometimes people mean well, but just don't think things through properly before saying or doing them. When someone does or says something that rubs you the wrong way, before instantly getting upset or angry, consider their intent. Haven't we all put our foot in our mouth at one time or another? I know I have, and it's the worst feeling when I hurt someone without meaning to. Show others a little bit of grace when they do it to you.

This reminds me of the time when baby Catherine was less than a year old, and I was carrying her in her car seat into the daycare one morning before heading off to work. An older kid and his mom were behind us and followed us into the building. I signed her in at the front desk and headed to her classroom to drop her off. I bent down to take her out of the car seat and saw something purple in and around her mouth. *That's weird*, I thought. I pried open her little mouth to investigate what in the world was in there and realized with horror that the little boy must have picked a flower out of the daycare's garden and handed it to her. And since she was a baby, of course, she put it in her mouth. Because the car seat was facing behind me, all of this happened without me realizing it!

You know me well enough by now to know that I totally freaked out. Was the flower poisonous? I ran to the daycare director's office, but she wasn't in yet because it was so early. I desperately tried to find out what kind of flower it was to make sure it wasn't poisonous, and I called the poison control center and described it to the operator. (It didn't occur to me to just Google it.) After an emotionally exhausting half hour, we all came to the conclusion that it wasn't anything to be concerned about, and she was fine, but what an unbelievable way to start the day.

My point? That little boy was just trying to be kind when he gave her that flower. Even though my initial reaction was one of terror that my daughter could be in danger, I knew that he wasn't trying to do any harm. I calmed down, looked at the situation in its entirety, and got through it with a (relatively) level head.

Can I Help You?

Another way that I get bursts is by helping people. A desire to help others has always been who I am, so I actively find ways to do it. At the moment, writing this book is bringing me happiness because I'm hopeful that it will bring more joy to people's lives. Way back in kindergarten, I remember how every morning on the bus ride to school, I would pray to the dairy gods and the gods of Richneck Elementary School that I would be chosen as that day's milk helper. The person in this highly sought-after position would survey the class, find out how many people wanted plain vs. chocolate milk, collect the money, go to the cafeteria to make the purchase, gather the milk cartons, and deliver them to classmates. I lived for it, and I'm sure my teacher must have known how much it meant to me because it seemed like I was selected every other day. It was awesome.

Present-day Lisa still gets fired up every time she helps someone, so I'm always looking for opportunities to be of service to others—like the time a few months ago when I was at the grocery store. I spotted an older lady in the produce department next to the broccoli. She was struggling to open one of those produce bags to put it in. I strolled over and asked if I could give her a hand. She was very appreciative, and as I got it open for her, we exchanged general pleasantries. I handed her the opened bag (and a few additional ones in case she needed them for more vegetables) and told her to have a great afternoon.

The whole interaction lasted about ninety seconds, but I felt amazing afterward. It was the adult version of the milk helper! I felt so good about it that I even had to talk myself down afterward: *Take it easy, Lisa. You didn't just save her from choking, for crying out loud.* It was a little thing, but I felt the same warm and fuzzy feelings that I did when I was the milk helper. Helping others makes me a happier and more authentic version of myself. Whenever I'm able to help out a fellow human being, I get all the feels, so I intentionally seek out opportunities to do it in order to create more bursts.

My Challenge to You

What brings you joy and fires you up? Think about how you get yourself out of a crappy mood. When you're at your happiest, what are you doing? Reading? Singing? Drawing? Painting? Running? Use that information to discover the ways you can add more bursts to your life on a daily basis, and then figure out how to do them more often.

Drawing a blank? Think back to what you were like as a kid, or talk to someone who knew you back then. What made you happy when you were little? Perhaps there's still a trace of that passion in you. Were you athletic? Does the idea of signing up for a class at your local gym, or registering for a five km run create some excitement in you? Have you always enjoyed writing? Maybe start keeping a journal, or decide to write that book you've had in the back of your mind for years. Are you crafty? Do it more often! Do you love singing? Turn off the podcasts you usually listen to in the car on the way to work and occasionally listen to music instead, or maybe even join a choir. Are you a performer? See if your community theater is holding auditions for a production.

Are you in the thick of it with little kids at home? If you miss spending time with your friends, make the effort and do it! Line up a sitter and spend an evening out. It'll be wonderful to not have someone physically hanging on you or throwing food at you while you try to eat, and you can finally relax and enjoy a meal and have some adult conversation. If you want an evening out, make it happen.

Come up with some ideas, see what excites you, and then find ways to insert those activities into your life as often as you can.

Are there opportunities to incorporate more bursts into your professional life? If you don't love what you do, is it time for a career change? If that's not possible, consider volunteering for a cause that's important to you. You'll get bursts by contributing to something you believe in while also making a difference in the world.

Do you manage a team at work? Think outside the box to create more bursts for your employees while also benefiting the organization. According to the job matching website Localwise, while you may be busy instructing employees on what to do next, it's important to get to know them. Understanding employees as individuals is key to understanding which areas they excel in, and how you can utilize their passions to help your business grow.[3]

Burst of Joy #7:
Kindness at Work

WE'RE HUMANS FIRST AND COLLEAGUES, CLIENTS, CUSTOMERS, AND COMPETITORS SECOND.

Speaking of work, kindness matters professionally too. Creating bursts for your colleagues will lead to healthy professional relationships. It doesn't mean becoming BFFs with everyone you work with; it simply means showing respect, courtesy, and building human connections. Many years ago, I had just started a job when a colleague's sister was in a terrible car accident and was in the hospital for weeks. Of course I wanted to help somehow.

Since she would meet her family at the hospital every evening after work, I figured I could provide them with dinner one evening. Close to the end of the day, I ran to the grocery store before she was planning to leave for the hospital and returned with a bucket of fried chicken for her to bring along. Did it help them that day? Sure, it was probably helpful that they didn't have to eat the hospital cafeteria food for the twenty-fifth day in a row. But I like to think it was also the fact that someone cared enough to go out of their way to help. That one act of kindness on my part built the foundation for a great long-term professional relationship.

Sometimes a bucket of chicken does more for the soul than it does for the stomach.

And it's not just with colleagues that you want strong bonds with—building positive connections with others in your professional sphere (vendors, suppliers, partners, and even competitors) has an impact too. That's right, I said *competitors*, and here's a story to back that up.

I had a friend who worked in an apartment leasing office. One of her responsibilities was to call competitors each month to get their current rates. Everyone hated this aspect of the job, but it had to be done. After years of regular phone calls with a gal named Amanda from her closest competition down the street, it was clear that the two women had the potential to become friends, but she didn't want to make it weird. During one of their rate inquiry calls, Amanda opened up to her about having a hard day after a death in her family. That night, my friend bought a card for Amanda with lovely words about hope and healing, and she took it to her office the next day. A few months later, this former competitor helped my friend to get a job with her company, proving that small acts of kindness don't go unnoticed. We all know that building solid relationships within and outside one's own organization is a smart career move, but it's also a great move in terms of bridging differences between people and ultimately making the world a little bit brighter for others, and for you.

Stories involving the power of kindness are important to share. Whenever I have the opportunity to speak to groups of soon-to-be or recent college graduates, I tell them the story of Ernie. When I had David almost twelve years ago, Ernie mailed a box filled with baby goodies to the office to congratulate me on his arrival. He was a vendor I had worked with on a few small projects, and I hadn't even connected with him in years, but it was such a kind thought, and I always remembered it. Yes, I know that he probably didn't pay for it out of his own pocket, but it didn't matter. He went out of his way to congratulate my family, and my husband and I felt a burst of joy from his kindness.

As a result of this experience, I explain to these young adults that they may be given a line item in their budgets to purchase small tokens of appreciation for existing clients, prospective clients, vendors, and others that they work with, which is intended to help build relationships. Spend that money, I say! If they don't have a budget for appreciation gifts, I encourage them to buy a package of cheap blank note cards, and to send simple notes of acknowledgment to people when they're going through happy or tough times. Those small gestures of kindness will make an impact and won't be forgotten.

Obviously, kindness is the secret sauce to getting and retaining clients and customers. Author Bob Burg internalizes the golden rule of sales by reminding us that "all things being equal, people will do business with, and refer business to, those people they know, like, and trust."[5] After the roller skating incident, my wonderful family and friends were quick to jump in and help me with whatever my family and I needed, but what surprised me was how many of my work colleagues and business connections also reached out to offer an extra hand too (since I was down one). It was very cool.

It Can Get You the Job

I found out a year after starting my first professional job after college that I got the job in part due to my kindness and positive energy. At the time, I was twenty-two, bright-eyed, and eager to get into the real world and start making real money. I don't remember much about the interview, but obviously, it went well enough to get the gig. A year later, my boss casually mentioned that the final decision as to who would get my job had come down to a choice between one other candidate and me. Both of us were equally qualified and could do the job, but in the end, my friendliness, enthusiasm, and positivity tipped the scales in my direction. I always remembered that and knew there was something there, and whenever I have the privilege of speaking with young people, I share this life lesson with them:

Kindness matters . . .
~~even~~ *especially* in the real world.

Aside from just being a good human being, acting with kindness can also make you stand out from the competition and give you an edge. This isn't a new concept. Virgin Group's legendary founder Sir Richard Branson runs an empire made up of 200 companies in everything from healthcare to hotels to space travel, and he credits much of his success to one thing: hiring the right people to build unstoppable teams. The first thing he looks for in a great hire is personality, saying that it's the most important quality for a successful business; employers can always teach job-specific skills and company knowledge later.

Further, he says, "We look for people who are friendly and considerate, and who like working with others. From our airlines to our call centers, and our office buildings to our gym floors, you will always see smiling people working together to get the job done. These personalities make our staff successful, and, in turn, our businesses successful."[6]

**Skills can be taught,
how you make people feel can't be.**

My Challenge to You

It's easier than you think to spread bursts of joy to people you don't know. A friend recently posted to Facebook that a guy standing next to her at church complimented her on her beautiful singing voice at the end of the service. She didn't know him, but the fact that he complimented her made enough of an impact that she shared it on social media. It made her feel good about herself, and it took only two seconds for him to compliment her.

Commit to brightening someone's day on a regular basis with a kind word, smile, or compliment. Simple expressions of kindness have more impact than you think. If we all did just a little bit more of it, imagine the results! What we would have is a society filled with more optimism, hope, and feelings of connectedness. Think about it: each of those people goes home to their families, connects with their friends and colleagues, and interacts with tons of strangers when they're out and about. If they experience kindness more frequently, they'll start to feel more joy, and that joy will spread like a virus. And joy, unlike COVID, is something we *want* to spread.

Burst of Joy #8: Friends (the people) and Family

"Family is not an important thing. It's everything." — Michael J. Fox

I won the family lottery, especially when it comes to Jonathan. As you know by now, I'm married to an amazing man. He's kind, funny, smart, and as you read earlier about how bad my issues were at one point, he's also incredibly patient and understanding. We're going to be celebrating our twentieth wedding anniversary in a few months, and it's been a great ride. Of course, there are times when we just don't see eye to eye, but those times are pretty few and far between.

I have to admit that it was a little bit bumpy when we were looking to buy a house. We knew what we wanted: four bedrooms, a finished basement, a spacious backyard, etc. There were a couple of houses that didn't quite meet those requirements, but I liked them anyway. Jonathan would remind me that they didn't work for us because they didn't have x, y, or z, and my response was, "But I *feel* the love in this house!" How does one argue with that non-logic?!

On paper, our relationship should not work; he's the exact opposite of me in just about every way. In fact, on the Myers-Briggs personality test (which identifies an individual's psychological preferences in terms of perceiving the world and making decisions), we are the exact opposite in every single category. (I'm an ESFJ, he's an INTP, meaning to my "extraversion" he's "introversion"; to my "sensing" he's "intuition"; to my "feeling" he's "thinking," and to my "judging" he's "perceiving.") But somehow, it works. I think it's because even though we're different when it comes to a lot of stuff, at our core, we're very similar. We share the same values and basic beliefs, and we respect each other.

During that first date inside that huge Ruby Tuesday booth, he told me that his dream was to live in Colorado someday because of his love of the mountains. My response? "Good for you, buddy. I hope that works out for ya." I was very content living in Newport News, Virginia, where I was born and raised and where my family lived. Fast-forward a year later to him proposing marriage. After I said "yes," my next thought was, *Oh crap. I guess I'm moving to Colorado.*

Three years later, we made the move out West, and it's been great. Over the years, I've always tried to create bursts of joy for Jonathan, and he for me. (Although we never officially called it that, it's what we have been doing all along.) When we first moved out to Colorado, I was chatting with someone at work, and off the cuff, he mentioned that his neighbor owned a lot of heavy machinery to maintain his extensive garden. Apparently, this guy had a huge property and lived in a rural area. Suddenly, I remembered the stories I'd heard over the years about how much Jonathan loved digging holes in his backyard when he was a kid. His mom told me that he would be back there from sunup until sundown, just digging holes. Without even thinking about it, I asked my colleague if his neighbor had a backhoe in his collection.

He did, so I immediately asked for the gentleman's phone number so I could call him (these were the days before texting) to ask if he would be willing to let my husband live out one of his dreams of operating a backhoe to dig the biggest hole he's ever dug! I called this kind man the next day to ask, and he generously offered to make it happen.

Of course, if this happened now, I could have put the request out on social media and probably found someone willing to let us do it, but this was back in 2003/04, well before any of that existed. Stuff like this had to happen organically, or by making connections

97

with friends of friends of friends. I guess I could have searched for a place to rent out a backhoe, but we were just starting out and didn't have money for that sort of silliness. Long story short, this very sweet man allowed me to surprise J with his lifelong dream.

I kept it a surprise, and even on the appointed day, I didn't tell him where we were going. As he drove, I gave him directions *(that I had in my hand because it was printed out on a piece of paper)*. As we got closer to the man's property, I could see the backhoe, and a feeling of excitement flowed through my veins. Jonathan saw it too. A smile slowly appeared on his face as he asked, "Am I going to get to dig a hole?"

My response, "You bet you are!" And he had a blast. For thirty pure minutes of joy, Jonathan dug a hole. He could now cross that one off his bucket list.

Creating bursts of joy for friends and family doesn't have to take a lot of time or money. It just takes a bit of thought.

I am not the only one in our partnership to experience the benefits of seeking out joy and recognizing that what we enjoy can change over time. Jonathan has also definitely evolved when it comes to discovering the things that bring him happiness. Nowadays, he's really into ice and mountain climbing; nothing makes him happier than to be out on a mountain doing his thing. I have no desire to do it too, so thankfully, he has a wonderful network of people who do that sort of thing with him. This hobby means that he's not home at least one day out of each weekend, with the occasional weeklong climbing trip mixed in.

Some of my friends ask how I'm okay with him being gone so much. Well, quite frankly, it brings him tremendous amounts of joy, and I know how important it is to him. Honestly, though, it's a lot easier now that our kids are older. It was much harder when they were in the baby and toddler phases: he didn't get out much during those days. I want him to do what brings him joy, and this does the trick. A few years ago, he had an emergency appendectomy and couldn't go climbing for a couple of months while he recovered. He was a grump, and I couldn't wait for him to get back on the mountain, showing just how important this activity is to his well-being.

Jonathan creates lots of bursts for me too. Right now, he's creating a huge burst by encouraging me to go for my dream of making the world a bit brighter by inspiring others to live happier lives. I felt pulled to leave my regular forty plus hour a week job in order to write this book, create and maintain a blog (www.thejoyseeker .com), and go into professional speaking, all with the goal of helping others. He is behind me 100 percent and more supportive than I can say.

My friends are awesome too. Last week, Barry Manilow appeared on the *Today Show*. An hour before the segment with Barry, NBC must have promoted it before going to a commercial break because I received eight texts from eight different people at the same time to let me know. Thanks to their kindness in reaching out to me, I caught the appearance, and I loved it (of course).

One of the commonalities I'm noticing within my circle of friends is that some of us are struggling with feelings of inadequate parenting through this COVID fiasco. So many of us had the best of intentions. I, for one, planned on using this quarantine as incredible family time! We were going to play board games, watch movies together, and make lots of fun memories. Yeah, that lasted about a week. Once reality set in and life became like *Groundhog Day* with the same thing every single day, it got old really fast.

Factor in Jonathan and me trying to work while overseeing the kids' remote learning, the fact that they can't visit or play with their friends, and the only people the four of us see all day every day is each other, it all makes us want to have nothing to do with each other some days. One of the worst parts was that for a while, I was too nervous to order restaurant delivery for fear of germs, which meant I was cooking every single meal every single day. Not cool, COVID! Not cool at all.

Friends are saying that they feel like they're failing their kids by letting them have hours and hours of screen time, not interacting with them as much as they think they should, and not being completely engaged in their schoolwork and remote learning.

When they share these feelings, the first thing I do is assure them that they're not alone. There's comfort in knowing that others are responding in similar ways.

The second thing I do is tell them about Nancy, because if there was ever a time to Nancy something, it's now. Sometimes good enough really is good enough, and this is absolutely true right now. We're all in survival mode, just doing what we have to do to get through this. I commiserate with them that my kids are also watching a ton of Netflix, playing a crapload of *Minecraft,* and binging on so much YouTube you'd think it was their job. (I've also told my kids that this is all temporary and that once things are somewhat back to normal, this will not continue.) By sharing the reality of my quarantine experience, I remind my pals that we're all struggling and to try not to be so hard on themselves.

Parenting is hard enough; parenting through a pandemic is preposterous.

My Challenge to You

Think about what's going on in your family and friends' lives. How can you create occasional bursts of joy for them? Remember, it doesn't have to be expensive. Just look for opportunities that you know will make them smile.

For example, do you have a friend who is starting a new job next Tuesday? Make a note on your calendar to send her a quick text that morning to wish her luck. Have a friend who loves the *Outlander* series as much as you do? Forward her that James Frasier meme, and tell her to have a great day! Have a friend who just had back surgery? Bring over a bucket of chicken (or whatever she eats) or set up a meal train for her family. Have an out-of-state friend you haven't been able to connect with because of the time zone difference? Mail her a little card letting her know that you're thinking of her. You get the idea . . . It's just about taking a minute to let someone know that you're thinking of them.

BURST OF JOY #9: PARENTING

"I'M ALLERGIC TO POT ROAST." — CATHERINE WHITE, AGE SIX, WHEN TOLD WHAT WE WERE HAVING FOR DINNER THAT EVENING.

I love my kids more than life itself. Before having them, I assumed that my love for them would be like any other kind of love out there. Yeah, it's not. It's ridiculous how much I care about them and their well-being; how I would literally walk through fire to protect them from harm. They have brought me so many bursts of joy that I could fill up five entire books if I tried to share even half of them with you. The sweet innocence they have when observing and experiencing life is amazing, and the things they say or do crack me up so much sometimes.

Like the time we were potty-training David . . . He was doing great and was only having to wear Pull-Ups at night. To try to get him out of them, we made a deal with him: every morning that he woke up with a dry Pull-Up, we would give him some candy. The next morning, he ran into our room to show us his dry Pull-

Up! Great job, buddy! Here are a few M&Ms. The next morning, the same thing. And the day after that. We were on a roll! I told his daycare teacher of his accomplishment, and we all praised him and cheered.

On the third morning, I started to smell something foul coming from his closet. You guessed it: he was taking off the dirty Pull-Up each morning, putting a clean one on, claiming victory, and collecting his candy. He was scamming us! Of course, we told him that was unacceptable, but if I'm totally honest, I had to respect it a little. What really made me laugh, though, was his belief that we would never find out—that those stinky, pee-filled Pull-Ups would magically disappear. So funny.

A couple of years later, it was time to think about him starting kindergarten. Where we live, school starts in August of each year. Since he has an August birthday, we had the choice of either starting him when he was four (he would turn five two weeks after kindergarten began) or waiting a year for him to start when he was a couple of weeks shy of turning six. He'd been in daycare since he was an infant, so he was familiar with the structure, listening to teachers, and interacting with other kids. After talking to his daycare and preschool teachers, we all felt that he was ready, so we had him go earlier.

On the afternoon of day two of kindergarten, the teacher sent me an email with the subject line "an incident." *Oh, dear,* I thought. *This can't be good.*

Apparently, David got tired of waiting for another student to finish using a marker that he also wanted, so he took it from him and scribbled on this kid's forehead with the said marker. When the teacher asked David why he did that, his response was "because he was taking forty years with it."

Of course, I immediately thought that I made the wrong choice and that David wasn't ready to be in kindergarten after all. Thankfully, it was an isolated incident, and he's had no other major problems since.

**"Raising kids is easy, civilizing them is not".
— Jonathan White**

One of my favorite Catherine stories happened when we were on vacation in Hawaii a few years ago. She was five and just loved the beach, so much so that it wouldn't surprise Jonathan or me if she leaves Colorado and moves to Hawaii the day after she graduates from high school. We were driving the Road to Hana on Maui, a sixty-four-mile-long stretch of very twisty road with one-lane bridges filled with beautiful cliffs and breathtaking waterfalls. As lovely as it is, for those who suffer from motion sickness, it's not so great.

Poor David was sitting in the back seat next to Catherine, turning a horrible shade of green as he felt a wave of nausea with each turn the car made. We were trying to pull over as quickly as we could, but we didn't make it in time, so he grabbed a sand bucket that had been tossed on the seat next to him and puked his little guts out into it. As he was puking, Catherine piped up and said in a very chipper voice, "Nothing's going to ruin this vacation!" Apparently, not even her brother losing everything he ate that day. I hated to see my boy not feeling well, but her response was so freaking funny that Jonathan and I could not stop laughing.

Another fun Catherine story happened last Christmas, when she wrote a very compelling letter to Santa telling him what she wanted. She is one smooth talker, and even at her young age, she recognizes the importance of making others feel good about themselves, even if it's a bit manipulative in order to get what she wants. The following is what she wrote (edited for spelling and grammar):

> *Dear Santa, I have been good for the past few years. Can I have more presents on Christmas Day? You are the man who can do it.*

That kid is going to go far in life.

As fun as it is when they're little, I think all parents will agree that it's also incredibly exhausting. They're so needy and helpless, and we're at their constant beck and call. Yet, even though I vividly remember how hard those times were, I tend to get a bit nostalgic for those days. I

106

actually felt sad when Catherine finally grew out of diapers. Why on earth would I miss the disgusting diaper phase?! Throwing out that Diaper Genie should have been only a cause for celebration, yet I experienced a bit of sadness—especially since she's my youngest.

Why do I feel nostalgic? I think it's partly because time goes by so darn fast. Almost twelve years ago, we brought baby David home, and it feels like just yesterday. That eight-pound, fifteen-ounce little guy (yes, I have big babies) will be starting seventh grade next year. It's crazy! I think it's also because my kids don't need me as much as they used to. Last year, David was going to give a presentation at school that parents were invited to attend. As soon as I saw him, of course, my instinct was to give him a big hug and kiss. As I approached, arms wide open and my heart filled with love, he mumbled, "Don't hug me, Mom."

Ouch. Of course, I didn't take it personally. I get it: not wanting to be hugged and smooched on in front of your friends is a normal part of becoming a teenager. But I did make sure to give him extra hugs and kisses that evening in the privacy of our own home, whether he liked it or not. It shouldn't make me sad that they're growing up—after all, isn't that the goal of parenting? Raising them to be happy, independent, and self-sufficient adults means that you've succeeded as parents.

As they get older, instead of feeling a loss for the times that are over, I'm focusing instead on seeking out the joy that comes with each phase that they're now in. Each comes with its own unique set of joys, and there are lots of bursts to be had with a pre-teen kid. For instance, instead of having to play the mind-numbing Candyland game, David can now play Scrabble (which I usually win) or chess (which he usually wins). If we're out and about and have to go to the bathroom, I don't have to take him, and we can watch a movie that's not a cartoon and have a great discussion about it afterward.

Try not to dwell on the sadness of what's over when there's still so much joy to be had.

My Challenge to You

If you're a parent, try to enjoy each phase that your kid(s) goes through. Like me, a part of you may be sad that they're growing up, but the fact that they are means you're doing a great job!

Burst of Joy #10: Karma

Most of the time I care about others and wish the very best for them. Sometimes, not so much.

We can all agree that middle school is hard, representing some of the toughest years we'll ever go through. I was so incredibly awkward—always trying to fit in, but failing miserably. I look back at pictures from that time and cringe. I had this hot pink sweatshirt that I thought I looked amazing in (I wore it at least twice a week) and went with the poufy bangs and hair in a banana clip look. Not good.

In the sixth grade, a fella that we're going to refer to as "Jerk Face Jeff" was in my class, and we were pals. If I'm totally honest, I may have had a small crush on him. One day, I was sitting at my desk in homeroom, minding my own business, when all of a sudden, he started teasing me about my leg hair—out of nowhere! Now I'm Italian, so dark leg hair comes with the territory, and I was already self-conscious about it. The fact that Jeff noticed it and teased me for it in front of the other kids was traumatic. I went home and cried to my mom, begging her to let me shave my legs. She thought I was too young, but I pleaded, I bargained, and finally, I threw a tantrum. I eventually wore her down, and she told me to do whatever I wanted, so I did. Obviously, I was not pals with Jeff after that.

Jeff must have gone to a different school the next year because I don't remember seeing him after sixth grade. Fast-forward to college. I went to a small school (about 3,000 students) about three hours away from home. (Shout out to all the Longwood College grads out there reading this! Go Lancers!) All freshmen in the work-study program were required to work the dining halls, and in my sophomore year, I was promoted to a supervisor position, meaning that I managed the freshmen working in the program.

During the orientation, when we were welcoming the freshman class, I looked over and saw . . . Jerk Face Jeff. I couldn't believe it. I still knew his face—didn't even need to look at his nametag for confirmation; I was certain it was him. He must have had to repeat a grade or something since back in middle school, we'd been in the same grade, but now he was a freshman, and I was a sophomore. I moseyed over to him and introduced myself.

"You don't remember me, do you?"

"No, should I?" he responded.

"Well, you're the reason I started shaving my legs."

"What?" He looked very confused. I told him the story and how he teased me back in the day.

"I don't remember that," he said.

Well, I did.

He ended up being on my dinner shift twice a week. As the supervisor, I was responsible for assigning everyone their tasks for the shift. Most of the time, I would end up letting the employees decide what positions they would work during each shift, and usually, I would rotate it out to make sure everyone had to take their turn in the dreaded dish room. The dish room was, without a doubt, the worst assignment. It was like 200 degrees in there and required the unlucky employee to sort dirty cups and plates into the steaming hot dishwasher and remove them at the other end.

You see where this is going, right? I assigned "poor" Jeff the dish room for every single shift that he had with me that year.

You would think that I would have felt bad about that, but surprisingly, I felt zero guilt. If given that opportunity today, as an adult, I don't know if I would have been so callous and heartless about it. I like to think that I have evolved and wouldn't be so petty, but I'm not sure. The way I figured it, God handed me a golden opportunity, and I wasn't about to turn it down.

After a few weeks, Jeff recognized the predicament he was in. Before a shift one Tuesday evening, he approached me.

"I thought about it, and I think I remember you. I'm so sorry I did that and behaved that way all those years ago."

"Wow, thanks, Jeff. I appreciate that. Head on over to the dish room now."

"Oh, come on!" he shouted and stomped away.

**The dish room sucks,
but some people deserve to be in there.**

My Challenge to You

Trust the universe. And don't judge me . . .
I'm only human.

FAREWELL

I hope my story has inspired you to make the commitment to seek out and embrace whatever it is that brings you bursts of joy. Remember, just knowing what brings you bursts isn't enough. You have to put them into practice to make an impact. Be intentional about doing whatever you can to bring more joy into your life, and into the lives of those around you (except for those few who deserve to be in the dish room). Put them in there, and forget about them.

But for everyone else, you have more influence than you think you do in terms of making their lives a bit brighter. If enough of us make just a little bit of an effort, we can make a huge difference overall. Not only will the impact of your joy make you happier, but also it will spread to another and then to another and then to another, creating a ripple effect that will eventually lead to a collective shift in our culture. But it has to start with us. When people see us living with and experiencing more bursts of joy and they can see that joy spreading to others, it'll catch on. If we all do just a little bit more, imagine the results.

Let's do this.

NOTES

1. Dr. Tasha Eurich, *Insight* (New York: Penguin Random House, 2018), 18.

2. Dr. Tasha Eurich, *Insight* (New York: Penguin Random House, 2018), 4.

3. "21 Ways to Keep Employees Happy and Productive," Localwise, Accessed May 20. 2020, www.local-wise.com/a/1008-21-effective-ways-to-keep-employees-happy-and-productive.

4. Alex Dixon, "Kindness Makes You Happy…and Happiness Makes You Kind," Greater Good Magazine, September 6, 2011, https://greatergood.berkeley.edu/article/item/kindness_makes_you_happy_and_happiness_makes_you_kind.

5. Bob Burg, "All Things Being Equal," Accessed on May 20, 2020, https://burg.com/2010/04/all-things-being-equal/.

6. Vivian Giang, "7 Hiring Rules that Richard Branson Lives By," LinkedIn, August 29, 2016, https://business.linkedin.com/talent-solutions/blog/recruiting-tips/2016/7-hiring-rules-that-have-lead-sir-richard-branson-to-success.

7. Jane McGonigal, *SuperBetter: A Revolutionary Approach to Getting Stronger, Happier, Braver and More Resilient* (New York: Penguin Press, 2015), 39-40.

8. Jane McGonigal, *SuperBetter: A Revolutionary Approach to Getting Stronger, Happier, Braver and More Resilient* (New York: Penguin Press, 2015), 17-19.

ACKNOWLEDGMENTS

It's so strange that I'm writing a book about joy and happiness during a time filled with so much stress and misery. Several months ago, when this quarantine started, I wanted to come out of it with something positive, so I finally decided to write the book that I always wanted to write—a book that I hope and believe will help others, now and in the years to come. I still can't believe I actually finished it! It's a dream I've had for as long as I can remember, and if I help just one person feel happier and more optimistic, I've done my job.

To my fellow author and #SpeakerSister Tracey Ferrin, thank you for your encouragement, for answering all of my silly questions about writing a book, and for your support. You've been a huge inspiration to me, and I never would have started on this journey without you cheering me on.

My dear friend, Sara Reynolds, you are the first person I told outside of my family about my desire to make a difference in the world and dedicate myself to helping people. Thanks for not laughing at me, and for being so encouraging! I've always appreciated you, and I value our friendship so much.

My sweet friend, Rose Millerlile: even though we live on opposite sides of the country, I think of you often. Your kindness, understanding, and optimism have always been so inspirational to me. Thank you for being such a special friend. I love you so much.

Dr. Marnee Colburn, where do I begin? Thank you for helping me through some of the darkest times of my life, both when I was a kid and as an adult. I don't think you'll ever know how impactful you've been to me. You gave me the tools to face my fears and fight for a happier life, many of which I still use to this day. From the bottom of my heart, thank you for your kindness, compassion, and belief that I could get better.

James Dimino, thanks for being a cool brother, and for always being the kind and fun "Uncle Jimmy" to my kids. You're a great guy.

Pamela Moran-Christner, you're an amazing mother-in-law, and you raised a wonderful human being. Thanks for being a wonderful grandmother to my kids and for always encouraging and supporting me. I truly love you like a mom.

Charlie and Cathy Dimino, thank you for always being there for me, to support and encourage me both as a kid and as an adult. You are wonderful parents and amazing grandparents to my kids. I am so blessed and grateful to be your daughter.

My sweet Jonathan, you're a good egg. I love you a ton, and I am so happy to be able to share this journey of life with you. You're my best buddy—I'm so lucky to have you.

David and Catherine, I'm so proud to be your mama. I'm proud of the kindness, compassion, and empathy you show to others, as well as your great sense of humor and intelligence. I'll always be in your corner, I'll always have your back, and I'll always be your biggest cheerleader. You are my biggest bursts of joy.

ABOUT THE AUTHOR

Lisa Dimino White is an author, professional speaker, and blogger at www.thejoyseeker.com. She is a huge fan of kindness and positivity, and she is passionate about empowering others to find more joy in their lives. Originally from Virginia, she now lives in Highlands Ranch, Colorado, with her wonderful husband, Jonathan, and two terrific kids, David and Catherine.

ONE MORE THING

Get in touch—I'd love to hear from you!

Instagram: @LisaDiminoWhite

Facebook: @lisadiminowhite

TikTok *(I know, it's ridiculous that as a 43 year-old woman I'm on TikTok, but it's surprisingly entertaining):*
@lisadiminowhite

Join the conversation, check out my blog, sign up for my email list, or inquire about having me speak to a group or organization that you're affiliated with at www.thejoyseeker.com

Thanks for reading! Now go find your bursts!

Made in the USA
Columbia, SC
20 August 2020

15576041R00079